The
Story
I
Am

Roger Rosenblatt

The
Story
I
Am

Mad About the Writing Life

Turtle Point Press | Brooklyn, New York

Library of Congress Cataloging-in-Publication Data

Names: Rosenblatt, Roger, author.

Title: The story I am : mad about the writing life / Roger Rosenblatt.

Other titles: Mad about the writing life

Identifiers: LCCN 2019052259 (print) | LCCN 2019052260 (ebook)

Subjects: LCSH: Authorship. | Life in literature. | Authors, American—20th century—Biography.

Classification: LCC PS3618.O8336 A6 2020 (print) | LCC PS3618.O8336 (ebook) | DDC 818/.5403—dc23

LC record available at https://lccn.loc.gov/2019052259

LC ebook record available at https://lccn.loc.gov/2019052260

Cover Design by Alban Fischer Design

Interior Design by Misha Beletsky

Hardcover ISBN: 978-1-885983-82-4

Paperback ISBN: 978-1-885983-78-7

Ebook ISBN: 978-1-885983-79-4

Printed in the United States of America

for Jane and Garry
beyond words

Introduction

It figured, I suppose, but I never saw the matter clearly until I began assembling this book—just how often I've written about writing, the life of the writer, and the written word. Not only in essays but in memoirs, novels, and plays as well. And in a book I wrote on the art and craft of writing, *Unless It Moves the Human Heart*. The subject kept rearing its siren head. Maybe that's because it took me so many years before I was doing the creative work I'd hoped to do from the time I was a boy. The world of the writer was the world I sought. I wrote about it, wanting in. And once in, I continued to write about it because trying to describe the writing life can be as entrancing and confounding, not to say as satisfying, as producing a piece of work itself. Well, nearly.

So here are pieces on the satisfactions, sorrows, menaces, and pleasures of the trade—on craft, on teaching writing, on reading, on books and the world of books, on being a journalist, memoirist, essayist, playwright, and novelist—in essence, on all things connected, directly or tangentially, with the life of the writer. As wide-ranging as these pieces are, they also seem to fit with one another. One of the happy surprises of pulling this book together was observing its unity of tone and mood—as though I had been playing a few notes of music at a time, scattered over a great many years, and then heard all the disparate parts coalesce into one recognizable tune.

1

Music, specifically jazz, in fact, plays a part in these pieces. Alan Bergman, who, in a brilliant partnership with his wife, Marilyn, wrote the lyrics to such standards as "The Way We Were" and "What Are You Doing the Rest of Your Life," says he hears the words in the music. I realize that I hear the music in the words. I play the piano by ear, and whenever I'm working on something I try to discover the sound of it. As jazz is the art of improvisation, so is writing, at least the way I do it. I hunt for the next word as I hunt for the next note. If I make a mistake, I deliberately try to follow it with another mistake, to make something right out of something wrong, and I continue in this mysterious foraging, as if trying to recall something I never heard before.

A definite passion drives this effort. Some of these pieces were written forty years ago, some in the past year or two. They suggest the same literary inclinations and standards, the same goals aspired to, the same mixtures of exhilaration and exasperation. But running through all that is my pure, rapturous, if often unrequited love of the game—on display in the comic complaints no less than in the expressions of wonderment and appreciation.

My biggest surprise as I collected these pieces was to realize that they defined me as writer. I teach a course in the MFA program in writing at Stony Brook/Southampton called "The Story You Are." The course's premise is that every writer tells just one story over a lifetime. The story may take the form of a novel, a play, a memoir, a poem, or an essay, but it is always the same. In the music and common feeling of the pieces in this book I discovered my story. The theme of and reason for everything I've ever done were under my nose all the time, like Poe's purloined letter. I write simply because I am enthralled with

2

the writer's life, mad for it, and with the act of writing. Between the lines or in them, that is what these pieces say. The love of writing is the story I am.

I'm talking about the love of doing it, the love of process. I realize this marks me as an odd duck among some of my peers, who speak only of the miseries involved in stringing words together. Many of the best writers I know swear they hate writing yet are glad to have written. Not I. To me, the writer's life is an unending childlike adventure. Every morning you greet the day longing to tell the world something remarkable about itself. And even if it turns out that what you have to say proves less than remarkable, or the world yawns uninterested in your bright bulletins, still the prospect thrills you.

During graduation ceremonies at Stony Brook/Southampton, I tell my MFA students, "Welcome to the world of humiliation, rejection, and poverty." I don't mean it, and the students know it. What I really mean is, welcome to the world of your reckless imagining. The lurchings of your mind will defy common sense, including your own. Risk everything, gleefully. Seamus Heaney said it for the tribe: "Walk on air against your better judgment." It is another way of saying, improvise. Make the music your own and follow it into the dark. You sit at one or another keyboard, and something comes to you. And then you come to it, as if it were waiting for you all along. It was.

—RR

3

From the Memoir
Kayak Morning

The characters in a novel I'm writing have lost control of themselves. The one-eyed hag has become a two-legged dog who travels solo in a red cart and plays bluegrass on the banjo. The gatekeeper has become a beekeeper. He's so out of things, he tries to open and close a gate made of bees. He drinks. The hero of the piece is spread in a hundred directions like the roots of an old tree. As for the villains, there are so many by now, I'd be better off yoking them under a single name. This is what happens when you do not pay attention to the novels you write. Oh yes. And Death. A character called Death has stuck his Roman nose into the plot. He plays a vampire who needs a transfusion. It's a bad idea, don't you think? To give a transfusion to a vampire?

I sometimes wish I owned a shop instead, where I sold coconuts or objets d'art or Bowie knives—anything but books. People would come to my shop to get things they want. And I would give them what they want, and we both would take satisfaction in the transaction. The trouble with writing is that you give people what they don't want, and by the time they realize they needed what you gave them, they have forgotten where your shop is located. You, meanwhile, never noticed them in the first place. You were intent on your work, which consists of patricide and theft. I read Cavafy the other day, cover to cover, for the sole purpose of robbing his grave.

There's only one point to writing. It allows you to do impossible things. Sure, most of the time it's chimney sweeping and dung removal. Or plastering. A lot of the time, writing is plastering or caulking or pointing up the bricks. But every so often there is a moment in the dead of morning when everything is still as starlight and something invades your room, like a bird that has flown through the window, and you are filled with as much joy as panic. And then you think: I can do anything.

The Writer in the Family

So there I stood at the front of my granddaughter Jessica's fourth-grade classroom, still as a glazed dog, while Jessie introduced me to her classmates, to whom I was about to speak. "This is my grandfather, Boppo," she said, invoking my grandpaternal nickname. "He lives in the basement and does nothing."

Her description, if terse, was not inaccurate. For a time, my wife and I did live on the lower level of our son-in-law's house with him and our three grandchildren. And, as far as anyone in the family could see, I did nothing, or next to it. This is the lot of the writer.

You will hear someone referred to as "the writer in the family"—usually a quiet child who dresses strangely and shows inclinations to do nothing in the future. But when a supposedly grown-up writer is a member of the family, who knows what to make of him? A friend of my son-in-law's asked me, "You still writing?"—as if the profession were a new sport I'd picked up, like curling, or a disease I was trying to get rid of, like shingles. Alexander Pope: "This long disease, my life."

Writers cannot fairly object to being seen in this way. Since, in the nothing we do—the "nothing that is not there and the nothing that is" (Wallace Stevens)—we do not live in the real world, or wish to, it is fruitless and dishonest to protest that we do. When family members introduce us to one of their friends, it is always with bewilderment

7

camouflaged by hyperbole. "This is so-and-so," they will say, too heartily. "He's a great and esteemed writer." To which their friend will reply, "Would I have read anything you've written?" To which I reply, "How should I know?"

At home, they will treat us like domesticated, dangerous animals, pet pandas or snow leopards, patting and feeding us, while eyeing our teeth. Or they will make touching attempts to associate us with comprehensible pursuits, such as commerce. When he was three, my grandson James proposed that the two of us go into business together. "We will write things and we will sell things," he said, thereby yoking two enterprises that are rarely yoked.

Much of our familial treatment as weirdos is not only merited, it is also sought. We deliberately cultivate a distance from normal experience, whatever that may be. We seek and relish anarchy. One day, another writer and I were standing on a hill overlooking the irritatingly civilized village of Williamstown, Massachusetts. The sun was sunny, the flowers flowering, the air had just been sterilized. I remarked, "What I would like to see now is a gang of thugs stripping that car over there." My companion added, "With the church bells tolling."

The world of orderly decency, harmless ceremonies, and modest expectations, i.e., family life, is not the writer's. One morning at breakfast, when she was in the first or second grade, E. L. Doctorow's daughter Caroline asked her father to write a note explaining her absence from school, due to a cold, the previous day. Doctorow began, "My daughter Caroline . . ." He stopped. *Of course she's my daughter,* he said to himself. *Who else would be writing a note for her?* He began again. "Please excuse Caroline Doctorow . . ." He stopped again. *Why do I have to beg and plead for her?* he said. *She had a virus. She didn't commit a*

8

crime! On he went, note after failed note, until a pile of crumpled pages lay at his feet. Finally, his wife, Helen, said, "I can't take this anymore," and she penned a perfect note and sent Caroline off to school. Doctorow concluded: "Writing is very difficult, especially in the short form."

If the sad truth be known, writers, being the misfits we are, probably ought not to belong to families in the first place. We simply are too self-interested, though we may excuse the flaw by calling it "focused." As artists, writers hardly are alone in this failing. In Stephen Sondheim's masterwork, *Sunday in the Park with George* (at least the first act was a masterwork), we are shown the gloriously self-involved Georges Seurat dotting away at isolated trees and people in his all-consuming pursuit of the famous park painting.

Among those consumed by his zeal is his mistress—not technically family, but in the family way. He ignores her, leaves her high and dry. He's an artiste, after all. If one took a straw poll of the audience a few minutes before the first act ended, they gladly would have stoned the miserable son-of-a-bitch artiste to death. But then, in the very last scene, the separate parts of Seurat's painting coalesce before our eyes. Everything magically comes together. And the audience gasps, weeps in wonder. So who is the superior character—the man who attends to the feelings of his loved ones, or the artist who affects eternity?

Even when writers move to embrace the family, appearing to be one of the group, it is often in the interest of putting the group to use in their work. Alex Haley defined the family as a "link to our past," another way of saying *Roots*. For the wolf of a writer, the family is a crowd of sitting ducks. There they assemble at the Thanksgiving table, poor dears—blithering uncles, drugged-out siblings, couples at each other's throats—posing for a painting, though they do not know it. The objects of the writer's scrutiny may be as blameless as a day in Williamstown, but in the story he has in mind, the writer, being the freak he is, will infuse his family with warts and all, because defects make for better reading than virtues.

A few writers have expressed themselves on the matter of families, not always encouragingly. Reluctant high school students learn from Bacon that wife and children are "hostages to fortune." John Cheever, recalling life in the family he grew up in, remembered their backs. "They were always indignantly leaving places," he said. Margaret Drabble saw families as "dangerous." On the sunnier side, André Maurois, George Bernard Shaw, and Mark Twain lustily sang the praises of family life. George Santayana called the family "one of nature's masterpieces." Once you learn that line, you are not bound to repeat it.

See what I just did? I made a lame quip that only someone who knew Santayana's adage about repeating the mistakes of history would get, and even then, at best, the quip would produce a knowing smirk. And from whom? Another writer. Need I also mention the quotations from Pope and Stevens dropped into this essay earlier, just to show off? This is how precious, not to say annoying, we writers can be. By the way, as soon as Jessie introduced me as jobless and subterranean, I immediately thought of Ellison's *Invisible Man,* thus displaying yet another of the writer's antisocial features—romantic self-aggrandizement. In fact, the writer in the family is so out of things, so socially inept, that it may require an institution as basically benign as the family to take him in. We writers may be unfit for human consumption, but something about the malleable, permeable family structure says to us, "There,

There. That's okay." Of course, to further indicate how unfit we can be, we are perfectly capable of abusing that tolerance and calling it boring.

Whatever. The writer may not be good for the family, but the family may do wonders for the writer simply by teaching him that "It takes all kinds," including him. A generous view of the world may not be as artistically riveting as crazy acrimony, but it is a lot more pleasant to live with. (Who among us would choose Scott and Zelda as our folks?)

Besides, "It takes all kinds" is what the best of art says anyway, albeit with finer brush strokes. When Jessie introduced me, I watched her classmates for a reaction, either laughter or horror. There was no reaction whatever, not one bat of one eye. A man who lives in the basement and does nothing? And his name is Boppo? They treated me like family.

{ essay in *The New York Times Book Review* }

Dogstoevsky

The Dog. By Roger Rosenblatt. The dog barks. By Roger Rosenblatt. The dog barks by Roger Rosenblatt, who is trying to read *Crime and Punishment* by Fyodor Dostoevsky. He is trying to read *Crime and Punishment* by Fyodor Dostoevsky, but the dog barks. As Raskolnikov dodges his landlady, the dog barks. As Raskolnikov curses his sister's fate, the dog barks, too. The dog always barks. By Rodya Raskolnikov. *Dogs and Punishment* by Rodya Rosenblatt, by Roger Raskolnikov, by Fyodog Dogstoevsky.

Barkbarkbarkbarkbark.

I am not crazy yet. The dog has not barked me to craziness quite yet. All I have sought to do for the past two days, sitting in the same chair in the same house with the same chocolate kisses left over from Halloween at my same left hand; all I have sought is to make some progress with *Crime and Punishment.* It is a very great book. You ought to read it sometime. I ought to read it sometime. But the dog barks, so I cannot read *Crime and Punishment,* and so I have considered killing the dog, as Raskolnikov killed the two old women.

If you kill one dog, after all, what matters it to the balance of the world, if you know what I mean, and I think you do.

Of course, you do not hear the barking; you, swaddled

in the sweet silence of your Cadillac Escalade or your Library of Congress, you do not hear my Cairn terrier with the tommy-gun voice. Nor can you hear what my Cairn terrier hears. Nor can I. But I can hear *her*. It is a metaphysical riddle, is it not, that she barks at what she hears, but I can only hear her barking. Who then would hear the sound if I felled her with a tree in the forest? Bark to bark?

What gets me is how little she cares for my peace of mind. She has not read *Crime and Punishment*. She knows nothing of the pleasures of sitting back with chocolate kisses on a dismal November afternoon—the trees shorn, the wind mixing with rain—and reading of starving young Russians tormenting themselves in the city of_____, in the year_____. Six long years I have owned this dog, feeding and bathing and tummy-scratching, in return for puppy barking and dog barking. Now she is not six, I remind her. She is forty-two, older than I. Time to settle down, I remind her. *Tempus fugit. Cave canem.* (Barkbarkbark.) She is not the dog I had hoped for, not that dog at all.

Not that I was hoping for Lassie, if that's what you're thinking. Or Rin Tin Tin, or Yukon King, or Fala, or Checkers, or Him, or Her, or any dog that flies or takes fingerprints or says "Ruth" in bars. I was not expecting maybe Ms. Magic Dog of the Twenty-first Century, who would not only fetch me my copy of *Crime and Punishment,* but who also would have translated the book from the original. Not my dog. Not the dog of my dreams.

All I ever wanted was a good and quiet dog, like the dignified hound in Piero di Cosimo's *The Death of Procris,* sitting so mournfully, so nobly at the feet of his fallen mistress. A dog like that would not bark more than once a month. A dog like that would know his place in the order of things, would state by the mere fact of his docile existence that there are those who rule and those who sit quietly, those who read *Crime and Punishment* and those who don't, and therefore do not make it impossible for those who do, just because they hear things that those who do, don't.

Damn it, dog. Am I not king of the jungle? Am I not God's reason that civilization is not going to the Cairns?

Barkbarkbarkbarkbark.

There is nothing out there. I have been stalled on p. 71 for an hour, and there is nothing out there, while Raskolnikov has axed the two old women over and over again. He feels no remorse. What remorse would I feel—except to acknowledge in the foul tunnels of my heart that I am for whom the dog barks? That she barks to protect only me?

Now she is still for a moment. The brown blank eyes fixed with alarm. The head loaded, ready to fire. What can she hear? Is it the sound of an enemy I cannot hear yet? Or is it the sound of the enemy I can never hear, the sound of evil itself, of my own murderous impulse to kill the very dog who barks to keep me from killing the very dog who barks to keep me from killing me?

{ column in *The Washington Post* }

May I Kill You?

And what do you do?
I'm a writer. May I kill you?
What do you write, if you don't mind my asking?
I do mind. May I kill you?
Would I have read anything you wrote?
No. No one has. May I kill you?
That last novel of yours—what was it about?
Nothing. May I k . . .
And yet it showed promise. Or am I thinking of another writer?
You are.
I'm a novelist, too, you know. I wonder if I could send you my manuscript?
Of course. Please do send me your manuscript. But not by snail mail. Send it FedEx. So I can have it sooner. You know, I was remarking to my pet bat, Arthur, just the other night. I said, Arthur, I wish to God someone, anyone, would send me his manuscript. Or hers. I'd like to read the manuscripts in North America first, then extend my purview to the Baltic states and Indonesia, where, I understand, there are many more manuscripts.
Are you okay? You're sounding overwrought. Kind of manic. But I guess all writers are a bit wound tight.
Yes we are. May I kill you?
I must tell you, this piece of yours is great. But it's not for us.

Who is it for, do you think?

Can't say. It's just not for us.

Maybe it's not for anyone. What do you think?

I don't know. But I do know it's not for us. On the other hand, we really loved it and want to publish it as soon as possible.

You do?

Absolutely. Only, the first hundred pages? They have to go.

But the book is only 104 pages long.

Is it ever! We loved it!

What's wrong with the first hundred pages?

Nothing major. We can't tell who the main character is. And we don't know what the story is about. And we wouldn't be interested if we did. Do you see what we mean?

Absolutely. I could not agree more. I worked on the novel only six years, give or take, to pass the time. I knew it was shit. But you know how bored one gets. It was just something to do.

We understand perfectly. Would you like to kill us?

Would I! But not quickly. Crush your tongue in a vise. Pluck out your eyes with sherbet scoops. Sear your ass with a soldering iron. That's the way I'd like to do it.

I love your work.

You love my work?

It reminds me of Proust.

It does? Have you ever read Proust?

No. No one has. No one's ever read Proust. It's just something to say.

So you really *don't* love my work.

No, but I love Proust.

Me, too. May I kill you?

Know what I love best about your work? Its neorealism, that's what. And its neoplatonism, too. And its neologisms, they're the tops! I also love its lapidary style. Its catachresis.

Everything actually. The entire *oeuvre*.

Are you from *The New York Review of Books*?

Who isn't?

What did your review say about my novel? I forget.

We called it "lurid yet redeeming."

Ah, yes.

We also called it "lacking in style and content, yet brave." Personally, I don't think I've ever read a braver novel. How it fought off those other novels. Oh, see what I've done. I've hurt your feelings. Look. The trouble with you writers is you're too touchy. Too—how shall I put it—needy.

Why not say *needy*?

Needy. Yes. All you ever want is praise, praise, and more praise. And when you don't get it, you get all steamed up and pissed off. And you seek revenge. Revenge! Against *us*. You want to kill *us*. Other people. Why you don't even *think* about other people—unless, of course, we're praising you. Any other time, we're useless to you. Get real, will you? No one receives praise. That's the way of the world. When the guy gives you change at the 7-Eleven, do you tell him: "Hey man! Great change!" Planet Earth, me bucko. Your work may be brilliant or it may stink, and no one will ever know who you are, and you'll die and people will discover your unpublished stuff posthumously and say it stinks, too. Why should you care? That's not why you write. You write to *do* it. Isn't that so?

Do you mean that?

Certainly, I mean it.

You think we writers are destructively self-involved?

Duh!

Well, I must say. I never thought of it from your point of view. And what you say makes sense. I don't write for you, *any* of you. I write for me. Yes! This conversation has been a real eye-opener. Thanks. Thanks very much. Just one more question.

{ essay in *The Kenyon Review* }

Everyone's Work Is Magnificent

This rule applies to those occasions when people, often total strangers, have decided that you are the one person on earth to assess the merits of their oil painting, cooking, wood carving, sand sculpture, dress design, electric train setup, love song, or the 30,000-line tragicomic epic poem they have composed on the life of John Gotti, that they have never shown anyone until today. They "know what an imposition" their request is. But they seek your "frank opinion" because they "really respect your judgment." Here is your judgment:

"It's magnificent." Do not add a syllable. Shake their hand warmly, slap them on the back heartily, grin, and get out of there. If you believe that they wanted to hear anything other than "magnificent," you need a lot more help than they do.

{ from the instruction book *Rules for Aging* }

My Bear

My bear is of the polar variety. He squats at the other end of my kitchen table every morning, and he stares at me with his black, black eyes. He does not move, but I hear his even snorting. *Gnnn, gnnn, gnnn.* Like that, in a low guttural snort that is neither threatening nor amiable. If my kitchen window is open, the breeze will flutter the tips of his white fur. He is seven or eight feet tall (I haven't measured). There is nothing immediately alarming about him; yet, once I sit down, I am afraid to move.

He has something to do with my writing—anyone can see that. My fears. Or with my *not* writing. My blocks. Or with my mood swings. Once I suggested to him that he might be a bi-polar bear, but he showed no amusement. I offered him Frosted Flakes one morning, too. I do not think that bears have a sense of humor.

I cannot recall when he first appeared—some years ago, certainly. It was not in the morning that I first saw him but rather one midnight, when, for lack of sleep, I came downstairs for a snack of Jell-O, and there he was, glowing white in the light of a full moon. I sat and stared at him, as he stared at me. Eventually, I got sleepy and retired.

Lately, he has stirred from the kitchen, where he spends his days and has moved up to the bedroom at night, where he squats at the foot of my bed. He seems to wish to be with me night and day. I do not know what it is about me that attracts him. If he wanted to kill me, he could have done that long ago. Bears may look cute, but they are ferocious. One swipe of the paw and I would be scattered around the room like so many pieces of paper.

One night I decided to flatter him, but it made no impression. One night I presented a philosophical monologue to him—something that involved the fates of bears and men together in harmony. He did not so much as blink. One night I cursed him out. I don't know where I got the courage, but I even raised my hand to him. I hardly need to tell you that there was no reaction.

Here's my problem: If he establishes his influence in my household, as he has pretty much done already, how long will it be before he follows me outside? How long before he accompanies me to the newsstand or the grocer's? Think of the awkwardness, the embarrassment. He is not Harvey, after all, he's not invisible. And he is certainly not sweet natured or wise. Soon, no one will come near me out of fright.

I am thinking of calling the ASPCA. Perhaps tomorrow, or the day after that. My bear is an unwanted animal, is he not? It is the business of the ASPCA, their duty, to take unwanted animals and treat them humanely. I would not want him hurt. Yes, I will definitely call the ASPCA by the end of the week, or early next at the latest, and tell them to please rid me of my bear, my beautiful, big, white polar bear.

{ from the play *Ashley Montana Goes Ashore in the Caicos* }

From the Unpublished Novel
Young Murph

And do you know what's really great about the imagination? I said. No, tell me, Dr. Watson. What's really great about the imagination? Cait said, not even bothering to stifle a giggle of amused superiority. Well, I'm going to tell you, Holmes, you bitch. She laughed. The thing about the imagination is no one knows where it is located. No neuroscientist has the slightest idea where the imagination lives in the human brain. Mrs. Dwyer has this book about the brain, the areas of life it controls. Moving your limbs. Singing. Learning. Seeing. Hearing. All those functions, and more. Even loving. Every one of our activities has a home in some particular area of the brain. Not the imagination. The scientists concede the imagination is real, but they haven't found out where it lives. Most of them say it lives everywhere, in all the brain's regions. You know what I say? No, Watson, what do you say? She hadn't stopped smiling. I say the imagination is bigger than the human brain. It fills the universe. I say the imagination imagines itself.

The Writer's Wife

Look at him, my active man. Sometimes he sits and turns to the left. Sometimes, to the right. I wouldn't think of disturbing him. He is dreaming his writer's dreams, and his dreams are inviolable. I have the privilege of serving him, and of watching him.

Did you say something, dear? Nothing yet? Still dreaming? Well, while you're at it, I'd better get to my chores. No, don't get up. I can handle it: fix the engine on the Prius; recondition the Steinway; point up the bricks on the west wall; build a bathroom in the basement, from scratch. Busy, busy is the writer's wife.

And please, don't even think of lowering yourself to the details of bill paying, dry cleaning, shopping, cooking, dishwashing, trash toting. May I get the door for you? May I get two?

Am I complaining about my lot? Never, sweetheart. The intellectual challenges alone make it worthwhile. How many ways can I invent to assure you that you're not losing a step? Our topics of conversation: Your obligation to your gift. My obligation to your obligation. Were you born before your time, or after your time, or just in time? I forget.

Then there's our social life. The dinner parties where everyone speaks in quotations. The book parties where everyone says, "*There* he is. Or variously: "*There* she is!"

Do I want to go to Elaine's? Are you kidding? I want to live there!

And don't worry. I've laid out your uniform. Dark suit, dark shirt, dark tie. Your special look.

Do you think you might speak to me this month? It was so nice last month, or was it the month before that, when you asked me how I was. For a moment there, I thought you'd ask *who* I was. That's just a little joke. Nothing to upset yourself about. But what am I saying? Why would you be upset? Why would you—sitting there in your dreamscape—why would you even look up?

My folks, having met you but once, suggested I marry an actuary or mortgage broker. Or a wife beater. Hell, what do parents know about the life of the mind—yours. The precious moments we share—

Such as the times you asked me to read something you've written, and if I say "I love it!" you say I'm blowing you off, and if I appear disappointed or confused, you go into a clinical depression, and if I say, "Then please don't ask me, if you don't want my opinion," you go into a clinical depression.

Oh, dear. Did I say, "That was the best thing you ever wrote"? Of course, what I meant to say was, "Everything you write is a masterpiece. And this latest masterpiece just proves it." That's what I meant to say. You're right. I must learn to say what I mean.

Forgive me?

But soon we make up, and you'll say, "Let's go to so-and-so's poetry reading." And I'll say, "Oh, darling! Let's! Just give me a minute to freshen up and hang myself from the hall chandelier"—which, by the way, I repaired last week.

Memories? Say, rather, treasures! The day your agent

returned your call. The day your editor returned your call. The day you found your name in the papers. In the phone book. Remember the time we saw your first novel on sale in the Strand for one dollar?

How we laughed! The night you awoke with an inspiration for a story, and in the morning it sounded so silly?

Remember when I tried to write something myself, and you said it was "interesting"?

You know? I used to *like* books.

Ah. You've turned to the left again. I'm pooped just watching you. Watching you in your dreams. I dream, too. Here's mine:

Lord, please let him find a younger woman.

{ essay in *The Kenyon Review* }

25

From the Book-length Essay
The Book of Love

Tonight, I thought of you as the moon was turning its knowing face, the way you turn away from me at one of my contrived displays of wit. Embarrassed for me, who lacks the wit to be embarrassed for myself. Why is that? Why are you prepared to bear my slightest burden? I, the tropical ceiling fan, wheeling in my faux aristocratic self-confidence. You, with the serene sense to look beyond the slats of the casa shutters to the mango trees, the bougainvillea, and beyond those, to the sea. So steady, your eyesight. But tonight was different. The past had changed, as it does sometimes, and instead of the self-regard I have worn like a white linen suit, I saw only you, and the strawberries, and the windfall of light on your hair.

The story I have to tell is of you. It was related to me by a priest who had read it in an Icelandic saga memorized by an Irishman who recited it on a road packed with flutists and soldiers, where he was overheard by a young girl from Florida who transcribed it in a language no one speaks anymore. So I need to tread carefully. Stories like yours tend to slip away, if one is not careful. And I have been known not to be careful. A dead language is like the ruins of a great civilization. It glows as it is excavated. I shall tell your story in that language, whose power derives from not saying everything, like a poem. Or a song. Maybe a song.

The story I have to tell is of you. Of others, too. Other people, other things. But mainly of you. It begins and ends with you. It always comes back to you.

From the Memoir
Kayak Morning

Writing makes sorrow endurable, evil intelligible, justice desirable, and love possible.

Mash Note

Should we mix it up this Valentine's Day? I mean, a knockdown-drag-out, no-holds-barred, mano a mano donnybrook? You married a writer. You asked for it. Tell you what. Let's make love instead. Let's do both, and fight between the sheets. Does that make sense? Does anything about love make sense? Love is irrational, delirium, which is why neither of us would want to be one of those gods graced with eternal life, because if you have eternal life, why panic? Where's the fire? But if you're mortal, and are we ever, carpe diem, carpe whatever frantic impulse comes charging through your heart. So, what is it to be, baby? A shot to the kisser, or embraceable you? (I like a Gershwin tune. How about you?) Plant one on me.

The safest place to be in a tornado is a storm cellar. The safest place to be in a tornado is a railroad apartment on Bleecker Street or a Motel 6 or Williams-Sonoma or a bank vault or a North Korean prison. The safest place to be in a tornado is in your arms, you said, and you thought you meant it but you didn't. Love is no safer than a bread knife. Take the storm cellar. Tea for two and two for tea and me for you in a cottage small by a waterfall? I don't think so. Embrace the peril. If we're going to pick our song, let's make it "That Old Black Magic" and revel in the spin we're in.

How do conservatives fall in love? Conservatively, I suppose, like porcupines. Love may be better suited to liberals, for whom disorder is a work of the imagination. Within the blink of a black eye, you can be enthralled by me, disgusted with me, appalled, enchanted, smitten, bored (*Bored?* With *me?*), forever mine, forever through with me. Analyze that.

The trick is not to forget that we love each other, because couples do that. They forget to remember. As if love were keys to misplace or a purse to leave in an airport. What? Did I slip your mind? Did you slip mine? My irreplaceable you. Me sweet erasable you, you'd be so nice to come home to. That is, you or Tracey the waitress with the boobs I glimpsed in Applebee's last Tuesday. Unforgettable, that's what you are not, unless I concentrate on you.

Pope John XXIII said life is a holy mess. Is that so? Is the Pope Catholic? Life is a holy mess. Love is a holy mess. You were not meant for me. I was not meant for you. Yet there we were in the snow, our first night together, the quiet luster of you, composed like a Gershwin tune, like "Embraceable You," while I, a whooping rhinoceros, stomped about in boots, a rhino in boots, until we stopped, stood thigh to thigh, looked up, and caught the moon between the tangles of the clouds. My heart fell open like a knot.

Be my valentine in a blizzard, where the air is so thick, we cannot see two feet ahead of us, and we flail about snow-blind, without a GPS. Be my GPS to the tundra, the Klondike, and I'll be yours. The outer world of fanatics hates at the drop of a hat. Let us love fanatically, unhinged. O, promise me nothing. Is that you standing before me in the whiteout? Come to Papa. Do.

{ from the book-length essay *The Book of Love* }

From the Novel
Thomas Murphy

A poem should consist of two parts rocks, one part daisy. 'Tis my opinion, anyway. If the rocks aren't in the poem, you won't be able to appreciate the daisy. And if you take out the rocks, so all that's left is daisy, well, that's all that's left. It's not so yellow anymore. It wilts. You want hard language to convey soft thought, because in the end all poetry is about love, and no one wants love without a backbone. It's about contrast, see. The kiss and the slap. Oona and I never fucked so brilliantly as when we'd gone at each other beforehand, really torn each other up, tooth and claw. Then we'd hurl ourselves into bed and make a poem.

Essays. I, Too, Dislike Them

The essay consists of one part poetry, two parts history, three parts philosophy, and no parts sex.

My point of entry is a young woman standing before you reading a book, waiting for a train. She wears a round straw hat girded by a thick blue band. Her sandals are open-toed. Her dress is white with a pattern of small yellow flowers. Her skirt stops at her knees. Her expression skitters between the quizzical and the serene. She never lifts her gaze from the pages of the book, and she shows no concern for the time, the station, the train, her eventual destination, or for you.

What do you think? Is she a vision from a painting by Degas? Is she Galatea? Is she the intersection of thought and space? A problem? A symbol? A doop de doop?

Is that bulge in your pants a thousand words long?

{ from the essay collection *Anything Can Happen* }

Humiliation, Mon Amour

The woman at the counter in Barnes & Noble had silver hair in a bun and a smile like breakfast. I was with a friend, for whom I was buying a copy of my latest book. I do this often—buy my own books for friends, then wonder why I'm broke. "May I take a moment to sign it?" I asked the smiling woman. "Did you write it?" she asked. "No," I said. "I just like signing books." Unmoved, she asked, "Is this your first book?" I shook my head no, and continued inscribing. "It must be fun to write books," she said. "Superfun," I said.

On the sidewalk, my dismayed friend said, "A bookstore! At least you'd think they would know your name in a bookstore!" I told her not to be surprised. I wasn't. I might have been surprised had I entered Barnes & Noble expecting the salespeople to drop their books like dishes, shriek my name, and rush toward me tossing confetti. But experience has taught me that hardly anyone in or out of a bookstore will know who I am, or care. I have learned to live fairly comfortably with my writer's humiliation, and have worn it like a second skin over my original thinner one. After all, humiliations are suffered by most writers most of the time. And—to express a thought about life in the real world, for once—a writer's humiliations are chicken feed as compared with those endured by people who work for a living and are grateful simply to make it home at night. Writers are already home.

Naturally, some stinging recollections rise out of the past from time to time, such as that evening at a book fair in Providence, Rhode Island, when I stood beneath a golden banner with my name in red lettering, misspelled. It would have bothered me less had the banner not been provided by my publisher. And that evening in Washington, DC, when I was seated at a table bearing a tall stack of my latest book while a dozen non-buyers ambled past, paused, picked a book from the stack, opened it, read a clause or two, and returned it to the stack. (Truth be told, there have been several such incidents.) And that afternoon in Miami, when I appeared for an interview specifically requested by a local radio station, and the interviewer began, "Who are you?"

Rodney Dangerfield: "Every time I get in an elevator, the operator says the same thing to me. 'Basement?'"

Not all humiliations experienced by writers are as in-your-face as the above. A novelist friend describes summer workshops, where writers often squirm in the light of excessive adoration, as petting zoos. And there is the peculiar form of degradation offered by Q-and-A sessions after a reading. The first time I appeared at the 92nd Street Y, a man raised his hand when I had finished what I thought was a moving and sensitive presentation, to ask, "Are you related to Yossele Rosenblatt, the great Ukrainian cantor?" I said I wasn't sure, but probably not. "Oh! Such a voice!" the man went on. I scanned the crowd, hoping for a change of topic. My book, for example. But no further questions were forthcoming. After a minute, the first man spoke up again. "You don't look a thing like him," he said.

The most disheartening readings usually occur in bookstores, where throngs often swell to three or four people, at least one of whom has shown up to take a nap, and another who has misread the store schedule and come to the wrong reading. In Boston, a woman approached me after the Q and A, her face tense with anguish and disappointment. "I thought you were going to be Alice McDermott," she said. "So did I," I said. Of course, you can always pack the house with your sister and her friends and theirs, but that sort of crookedness only exposes you to family ridicule, which is far more gleeful and long-lasting than humiliation inflicted by strangers.

But back to the sidewalk in front of Barnes & Noble, where I had evidenced such maturity and equanimity. That reaction was in fact hard-earned. It took years for me to learn not to take a writer's neglect or ill treatment personally, and years after that to actually embrace humiliation and make some use of it. At one New York book event, I was seated at yet another table (they always place us behind tables, like prisoners on visiting days), in a cavernous room, for the hypothetical purpose of greeting and chatting with my many fans. There were none. A few feet away, however, at his own table, sat Chris Matthews, the news anchor, who had just written a book of his own and was welcoming a line of devotees that, as far as I could determine, had started out in China. Initially resentful, I refused to look over at Matthews, who extended nothing but bonhomie to me, smiling and nodding graciously. Then, slowly and meekly, I smiled back. I had realized something. By assuming the mantle as well as the burden of his fame, Matthews inadvertently was doing me a great service. I regarded him as a reverse Jesus, who lived that I might die of embarrassment, but of nothing more serious.

My awakening offered more still. It is much better for a writer to be underrecognized than over, in terms of keeping one's head down, like the proverbial Japanese nail, so that one might observe the world unhammered and unimpeded. Abjure fame and avoid obscurity. But between those extremes lies the perch where a writer occasionally might do some good work. There's a Jack Butler Yeats painting I love, showing a wild celebration of St. John's Eve in western Ireland, with Yeats and J. M. Synge standing in the background, watching and looking small and out of the picture. Yet it was they who created the picture, and a good deal more. Writer, love thine enemy. That's what I say.

I have a book coming out next year, about love. Romantic love, parental love, love of friends, of nature, of writing, of love itself. I did not include my love of humiliation, because it's too weird. A love like that ought to be kept under wraps, lest it get too widely known and invite the slings of more humiliators than one can handle. Besides, I would hardly be the first man in the thrall of a lover who treats him like dirt. Yet I might be the least.

{ essay in *The New York Times Book Review* }

Nobody Is Thinking About You

Yes, I know. You are certain that your friends are becoming your enemies; that your editor, agent, publisher, your readers, and your dog are all of the opinion that you have lost your touch, that you have lost your mind, that you have nothing left in the tank. Furthermore, you are convinced that everyone spends two-thirds of every day ridiculing your efforts, your style of dress, commenting on your disintegration, denigrating your work behind your back. I promise you: Nobody is thinking about you. They are thinking about themselves—just like you.

{ from instruction book *Rules for Aging* }

From the Unpublished Memoir
Unaccompanied Minor

T he best days are the first to flee, said Virgil. But before they do. . . . The birthday party when I was six, and, after blowing out the candles, singing every word of "Blue Skies" for my small, bewildered guests. At age four, sitting at the concert grand beside enormous Miss Jourdan, the editor and novelist who lived upstairs with Miss Prescott, the Columbia University librarian, and Miss Cutler, the ceramicist. Playing "The Blue Danube" and "Londonderry Aire" by ear. The ladies' squeals of delight. Accompanying my dad on rounds, and winding up at the counter at the drugstore on Twentieth and Park, the two of us hunched over ham sandwiches and black-and-white sodas. Tracking earthworms in the park. Riding an inner tube in Long Island Sound, straight to Portugal. Pears in a wooden crate. A horse's neck, as he is about to take a jump. The sea captain's house in Chatham, with the ship's wheel in the living room. Snow piled like cake frosting on my bedroom windowsill. A road under a hard blue sky, and, though you cannot see it or smell the brine, the sea it leads to.

And my mother, having returned home from teaching junior high English in a school on Hester Street. And her mother, Sally, lounging around our gothic museum of an apartment in the late afternoons while I, the apple of their eyes, deployed brightly painted British soldiers in the Charge of the Light Brigade on the green bedroom carpet.

My grandmother, whom I called Giga, big face, black hair, singing "Look for the Silver Lining." And my mother brandishing a shawl, strutting around the bedroom, like Mae West.

And my mother's father, Joachim, whom I called Patta, getting off the Third Avenue El, and coming to our house from his sign-painter shop in the Bronx, and sitting at the end of my bed to tell me stories. I was five. And the night he sat there saying nothing, and I waited eagerly until finally he said in his pea-soup accent, "This time, you tell me a story, Raagh." And I: "But, Patta, I don't have a story to tell." And he: "Tell me something you did today."

So I told him about Mrs. Morris, who took a bunch of the neighborhood kids to Palisades Park that afternoon, and all the wonderful rides we went on, and the go-carts, and the Ferris wheel and the waterfall, and the little pond, which I stretched to the size of a lake, and the live alligator with two teeth, one gold, one silver, that chased me up a hill into a cave, where I hid beside a black bear, the two of us sitting very quietly, burying our faces in cardboard cones of cotton candy. And I saw Patta's look of amused attentiveness, in which I also saw the power of words. And I loved what I saw.

From the Memoir
The Boy Detective

I tell the story of my grandfather as if he urged me on my way. But I don't think it's so. More likely, it is one of those memories we find to create patterns and connections in our lives where none exists. In the sixth grade, I wrote a poem about George Washington saying goodbye to his troops. This was not in response to an assignment. I simply was moved to do it. And I wrote things for the school literary magazine, only one of which I recall—a monologue spoken by a lawyer who had deliberately given little effort to his defense of a black kid from the streets, because his client represented a lower social class. Pretty obvious stuff.

But actually becoming a writer? I think I was more impressed by the idea of a person who worked alone and did what he liked. I relished stories about writers, movies about writers, as I did about detectives. The very word thrilled me—*writer,* one who imagines all of experience and creates it again. All the world sits in awe of writers, I believed, the storytellers of the race. Best of all, a writer is invisible. He tracks you down without your knowing he's there. And he's *not* there. A book is published. The writer does not have to accompany it. Go, litel bok.

From the Unpublished Memoir
Unaccompanied Minor

My mother teaches me to read. I am two and a half. We sit together at the dinette table with a book between us. I remember nothing of that book, or of any of the others we read, but I still can feel her closeness, the fresh-roses smell of her clothing, and our intense conspiracy over words. In her early seventies until her death from Alzheimer's years later, my mother will show only the look of fear. She will appear anxious even in death. But when I am little and she is in her mid-thirties, she is the face of serene competence. There is nothing she can't do.

We make eggnog. She teaches me to stir the eggs and to pour in the vanilla. We sew on a button. We run the vacuum cleaner. We go shopping in the neighborhood. People acknowledge her and wave. She buys a baker's dozen of cupcakes at the Gramercy Bakery and explains that a baker's dozen mean thirteen. She takes me with her to the milliner. The shop is dead quiet, and the proprietor snooty. How do you like this one? my mother asks me, dramatically tilting what looks like a huge gray stuffed owl over her eyes. I giggle. We'll take a baker's dozen, she tells the milliner, who is unamused.

The Disease That
Takes Your Breath Away

My mother died last week, seventeen years too late, of Alzheimer's disease—though not technically, of course. Technically, Alzheimer's victims usually die of heart failure, pneumonia, or perhaps a stroke, since the symptoms of the disease and a series of strokes are indistinguishable. My mother died of some respiratory thing, technically. It might be said that she died because she stopped breathing. Now, I would like to start breathing again myself, having held my breath for seventeen years.

Yet, oddly, I am wondering what to do with spring this year—oddly, because I had been thinking about my mother less and less as her condition deteriorated, and as she grew less and less herself. A mighty impressive disease, Alzheimer's. It takes your breath away: first as it inflicts progressive shocks on the victim's system, and then, in the victim's relatives and loved ones, as it deadens feeling altogether.

Such fascinating stages. Initially there is a kind of troubled yet sweet awareness that the clock of the patient's mind is a few seconds off. Then an encroaching recognition of loss of function becomes less recognition and greater loss. Soon words and phrases are looped, like mad lines from a postmodern play; then Tourette's-like bursts, frags, some incomprehensible, some vile; then less of that, less of everything, until the mind is concentrated down to a curious stare. Even in death, my mother's face looked worried.

A junior high school English teacher, she lived for words. She gave me words. When dementia struck, what happened to the words in her head? Did a civilization become a mob? Did the words take a bow and exit one by one, like players in a stage performance, until just one word was left? What was that word, Mom? Tell me. I'll write it.

Dead now, dead for years. I ought not to think about her. I should be thinking of China and the returned air crew of the spy plane. I should be thinking about the Cincinnati riots. There is Tiger Woods to think about, and the start of the baseball season; Pedro vs. Clemens up in Boston the weekend of my mother's death; I watched, half watched.

I should be thinking of spring and April: T. S. Eliot, Columbine, Hitler, Shakespeare, Waco, taxes, Oklahoma City, Jesus, Moses, Al Jolson singing "April Showers." My mother used to sing that. She was born on April 1st, no fooling.

But I am not really thinking about her either. I am thinking about not thinking about her, and feeling neither guilt nor responsibility. Now, here's a feat for Alzheimer's: it takes guilt away from a Jew! If I converted to Catholicism, would I get some back?

I do not feel guilty about my mother. I did my filial duties, lovingly, for the most part. I do not feel responsible. Alzheimer's drops in from nowhere, like a mistimed curtain. You don't catch it because you went outside in winter without a hat.

The trouble is, I don't feel anything, save the shadows

of memories, and even they have to be reconstructed willfully.

One day, when the disease was new, I took my mother to lunch and remarked over coffee that we should do this again very soon. "Yes," said my mother. "But the next time we have lunch, we should invite Joseph Cotten." She spoke with great earnestness. "Why, Mom?" I asked, since neither of us knew the actor personally. "Because Joseph Cotten is remarkable," she said. "He can listen to your dialect and know exactly what part of the country you come from."

Getting into the spirit of things, I realized that she was thinking of Leslie Howard or Rex Harrison, both of whom played Shaw's Professor Higgins, and I suggested as much to her. She considered for a moment, then smiled in a kind of gentle acknowledgment of the correction and of the craziness of the thought in the first place. "Yes, that's right," she said. "I was thinking of Rex Harrison. But as long as we've already invited Joseph Cotten, I don't think we should renege." The story used to amuse me.

The thing about Alzheimer's is that if it lasts long enough, it takes away everything, not only by erasing the person you once knew but by erasing the you you knew, too, leaving two carcasses. When the disease started getting bad, I used to tell myself that while I could make neither head nor tail of my mother's ravings, still she might have been clear as daylight to herself. When she caved in to silence, I told myself she might be harboring pleasant, unexpressed thoughts. Eventually I stopped kidding myself. What I saw of her was what I got: a blank stone in a wall eaten away by rain.

Which is very much the way I am now. The people

around Alzheimer's victims suffer from secondhand smoke, and the worst of their secondary disease is that, after the long years, the one thought, the one plea that overtakes all others—all the resurrected laughter, the walks along the beach in Chatham on Cape Cod, the brassy imitation of Mae West's strut, the home-sewn Dracula costume at Halloween, the bewildered attendance at basketball games, the singing of "April Showers"—is: die.

And so she did. And it is spring. And because hope breathes eternal, even if nothing else does, I am wondering if my mother is somewhere up and about, breathing again, where the words are restored and the air and mind are clear.

{ essay in *Time* magazine }

From the Novel
Thomas Murphy

Noiseless, I have drawn up my straw pallet so that I might lie on the floor beside my dad's bed. Above me, he breathes like the polar sea. He floats in his sleep. I would like to ride the current with him—the two of us on a mare heading to deep waters, under the sea's sun. But he is alone in his dying, as I am alone in my living. I lie on my makeshift bed, my arms behind my head like angel wings. Every so often, I look up. He begins to appear as glass, as a glass ink bottle into which I may dip my pen. I dip my pen in my father and write what he tells me. And now I am reborn, a new child again, learning to make my way in the new world. What is a rock? What is a daisy? Hours pass and I crawl around the poem I write of him and me. Soon I pull myself upright, vertical man, and I write of that, as my father instructs me. Automatic writing.

Then it stops, and there are no further instructions, so I put down my pen and cap the ink bottle, resting my head on the parchment of his arms.

From the Unpublished Memoir
Unaccompanied Minor

I am not quite three. My father isn't home most Sunday mornings. He usually is on rounds. But today is an exception, and I am glad of it. I want to write a book. What's the book about? he asks. I tell him I need his help, because the book will be about the heart, and I know he specializes in diseases of the chest. I also need his help because I know how to make only a few letters.

You dictate, he says, and then tells me what dictate means. I like the plan, and I start talking, as my father writes down my words. The heart has two parts, I say. The good part and the bad part. I go on to explain how each part evidences itself. I conclude that the good part of the heart always prevails. The words I dictate cover half a sheet of paper, which my father hands me. You should keep this, he says. You wrote a book.

Fathers' Days

The first time I swam—I mean, all by myself, feeling only Long Island Sound beneath me, and moving, actually moving in that fearful, unnatural element that could take my five-year-old life away if I stopped moving—that very first time I did it, my father was not with me. Yet he had taught me to swim. Day after day at Compo Beach in Westport, Connecticut, he had stood waist high in the low-tide kiddy ocean, holding me about the middle like a magician proving there was no possible way his assistant could be supported, but supporting me surely, only relaxing his grip by the smallest degrees as he waited for the moment I would flip off like a tadpole on my own. As long as he was there, however, that moment never came. Feeling his support disappear, I would mount an inversely proportional panic, and by the time I was free I was lost.

But when he was away in New York one day, I swam, and immediately hollered to my mother to see what I could do. It was worth a holler. My parents had had a time with me that summer, especially after I'd acquired the inner tube, which, while it was no father, could still support me very well, thanks, way past the teenagers on the dock, and out toward Portugal. Every day at least once, one of my parents would turn to the other with an implicit "Where is he?," and immediately look due west for a bump on the horizon. Then up would spring my father, who in those days had plenty of spring. And I would be saved. I loved to watch him come for me, chugging like a sub, I seeing as much pleasure as disapproval in his eyes as he towed me home.

He would have liked to see me take my first swim, I know, and I also know that I never could have swum with him close by, and worse, that I probably unconsciously timed my big moment deliberately to disappoint him, or to show him up—to confound his pride and love. That is the why it is so difficult to write of fathers and sons. The relationship is a continuous wrestling match in which arms and legs and victories and defeats are indistinguishable.

Such as the time eight years later, when we were on a short family holiday on Cape Cod, and my father and I agreed to swim out to a float and back. Being thirteen, I had so much strength, I never thought about it. Yet my father kept up, his dignified crawl beside my splashy riot. When we reached the float, however, his chest was heaving as if in sobs, and so he rested on the float for a while like a beached fish, before very cautiously dog-paddling back, holding on to the rope that led from the shore to the float, and sometimes holding on to me. Mortality, he explained, being the last thing I wanted to hear.

Or such as the time I accompanied my eldest son, Carl, then six, to a playground.

While he shot baskets, I sat reading on a bench at a distance great enough that an outsider might not see the connection between us. So when a couple of big boys came over, they thought my son was unprotected, and took his ball away to play a game on their own. Carl did not protest, merely taking his shots whenever the ball rolled his way. And when I called him to me to ask, discreetly, if he wanted me to intervene and get his ball back, he said,

"No, Dad, I can handle it"—that also being the last thing I wanted to hear.

But you've got to hear it. Freud said it is a complicated business, the relationship of son to father. And I'm sure it is, since every father's son is different. Yet most of the time it seems a terribly simple thing: The father sees his past and present in the son; the son, his present and future in the old man; and both resent and celebrate their fate.

"You want to be free, don't you, boy. Well, who's free?"

"I am." (Insistently, followed by a million hours of shouting and needling, until the wrestlers, out of breath, slow down at last, and the match, while never totally finished, becomes careful and stately as if the combatants were wrestling in water, or in that dense blue fluid in the jar where the answers float to the top.)

After I was grown, so to speak, and had children of my own, and my father and I had worked out our SALT XXXV, and would meet in the summers, as world powers meet, to discuss this and that—then we were friends. At night, with everyone else asleep, we would sit together in the kitchen of some country house he rented, talking about the past and future, even talking politics, which took a long time to learn to do without explosions, and hearing the Atlantic in the long pauses. When we were ready to turn in, I would put away the glasses, but it was always he who locked the doors.

And when he died, and I realized that from then on it would be up to me to lock the doors, I wanted to say: Look, Dad, it was you who taught me to swim.

{ column in *The Washington Post;* essay on *PBS NewsHour* }

From the Memoir
Making Toast

My grandson, Bubbies (née James), sits in my lap in the den. He locks his hands behind his head when he relaxes. I do the same. We sit there in a lopsided brown leather chair—same pose, sitting in tandem, like luge drivers.

One evening, he points to the shelf to his left and says, "Book." He indicates *The Letters of James Joyce*, edited by Stuart Gilbert. It seems an ambitious choice for a twenty-three-month-old boy, but I take down the book and prop it open before us.

"Dear Bubbies," I begin. "I went to the beach today and played in the sand. I also built a castle. I hope you will come play with me soon. Love, James Joyce."

Bubbies seems content, so I "read" another:

Dear Bubbies,

Went to the playground today. Tried the slide. It was a little scary. I like the swings better. I can go very high, just like you.

Love,
James Joyce.

Bubbies turns the pages. I occasionally amuse myself with an invented letter closer to the truth of Joyce's life and personality:

Dear Bubbies,

I hate the Catholic Church, and am leaving Ireland forever.

Love,
James Joyce.

It tickles me that Bubbies has chosen to latch on to a writer who gladly would have stepped on a baby to get a good review.

I try to put back the book, but he detects an implicit announcement of his bedtime, and he protests. "Joyce!" he says. Eventually, he resigns himself to the end of his day. He puts the book back himself and quietly says, "Joyce."

From the Unpublished Novel
Young Murph

Black rain; a lifted latch; a clutch of goslings; sedge; smoke; slush; write it; a woman wades in wet grass, wipes muck from her ankles; lamplight exposes a shame; bluish slate and a dunghill (the smell, the smell); sand and silt and a slice of stone; earth-brown cobbles; fresh cream in a bucket; the slap of mackerel; write it; blood-tipped fingers; a grief, a gulf of darkness; boot prints in a riverbed, and burnt straw, and the red trail of a fox; a flutter of fish; who's the drowned girl; a wheelbarrow avoids a traffic jam of sheep, and slips into the sluice; ghost-fog; lovers' secrets divulged near a rusted anvil; harmonica music; and a red-eyed drunk stumbles down a footpath toward the skull of the sea; o beautiful girl; o beautiful glow-worm; a sow in the furrow; turf in the hearth (the smell, the smell); sunplay on cobwebs in a barn; a dog in the doldrums; a mouth full of sprigs; a burlap sack; a whip; drizzle on your face; a bike on its side in the weeds; mud on the handlebars; mud in your hair; mud in your eye; mud everywhere (the smell, the smell); write it, write it; the quilt; the face; the shroud.

From the Memoir
The Boy Detective

I magine what you know. Shelley said something close to that in his *A Defense of Poetry,* and I have appropriated the idea in my memoir course. In the early classes, I talked about the difference between invention and imagination—the difference between, say, inventing a horse that merely talks, like Mr. Ed, and creating a horse that has something to say, like Swift's Houyhnhnms that bear the burdens of civilization. The imagination has different levels. You can imagine something that has never been seen before. And you can imagine something that has always been seen, yet never in the way you see it. For that you need to dream into the object of your attention, to see the inherent nobility in the animal that has borne so much without complaint and to make that animal ruler of the universe. Imagine what you know, I tell my students, and what you know will become wonderfully strange, and it will be all yours. More truly and more strange.

To push this idea along, I give them short exercises for their dreaming. The first day of class, I brought in a pair of old sneakers, running shoes, tossed them in the middle of the seminar table, and asked the students to imagine the ordinary sneakers before them. One young woman produced a piece about a man in the apartment across from her, who left one sneaker in the hallway outside his door every morning, because he had but one leg, and he needed that one sneaker, and then he put two sneakers out at night, as if to indicate that the other leg existed. In another exercise, I asked them to listen to a piece of music and to write a piece on what the music inspired. Poetry, fiction, memoir, anything. I did the same for a painting. And for a flower: dream into a tulip. I asked them to write a piece from the point of view of a part of the body, and of a part of speech. You're a semicolon, a hyphen. You're a dash. Show dash.

I asked them to write a piece from the point of view of a machine, to dream into the machine. The students became a bathroom scale, two clocks, an iPad, several cars, a guillotine, a vibrator, and a tattoo needle that spoke in rapid stutters.

More dreams. I eat their dreams like candy.

From the Memoir
Kayak Morning

Kayak. Ducky word. You can kick it. Hack it. Whack it. You can knock it over. In Kansas, Kashmir, or Karachi. It comes back okay, like cork. K-A-Y-A-K. And me, lucky kid, propped half-cocked in the cockpit pocket of my palindrome.

I am a fan of nouns. I tell my writing students that if they need three modifiers to describe something, they've probably chosen the wrong something. The noun carries its own weight, and the right one will not be made prettier or tastier or more important by anything that decorates it. It has all it needs. It contains what Emerson called "the speaking language of things." The noun. The heron. The tide. The creek. The kayak.

The Giant Rat of Sumatra

For much of my youth, my passion for language centered on lines from movies. There were certain things said in movies—old ones seen on TV, or new ones—that I cherished. Things I knew I wanted to hear again and again. I sought to incorporate them into my life, which is to say that I wanted to work them into normal conversations. Friends would be conducting a perfectly sensible chat, and I would be listening, like a lion in the brush, for an opportunity to slip in a line from, say, *Beau Brummel* ("Who's your fat friend?") or *Double Indemnity* ("There's a widespread feeling that just because a man has a large office, he must be an idiot") or *Pal Beach Story* (as said by Rudy Vallee to Mary Astor: "You know, Maude, someone meeting you for the first time, not knowing you were cracked, might get the wrong impression of you." For that one, of course, one would have to wait to meet someone named Maude).

To be sure, this hobby of mine did not make me the ideal social companion, but this is how it is when career and popularity are in conflict. The "fat friend" line earned me the everlasting hatred of a plumpish boy in high school, who was standing beside a friend of mine when I tossed in my movie question. I tried to explain to him that I was merely quoting Stewart Granger as Beau Brummel when he was miffed with King George III, but the boy seemed uninterested.

The lines I chose were never the garden variety, such as "Louis, I think this is the beginning of a beautiful friendship" or "Frankly, my dear . . ." and so forth, but rather ones that had a special attraction for me. The other day I heard such a line in a movie called *Jack Frost,* in which someone who was attempting to rid the world of a colossal maniacal snowman, explained: "We tried blowing him up, but it only pissed him off."

For many years, there were two lines I had never been able to slip into any conversation. The first of these, I never did get in. It occurred in *Earthquake,* one of the disaster films of the 1970s, in which a man was stalking a young woman to do terrible things to her. One would have thought that an earthquake would have been enough to divert his attention, but he was determined. At the height of the quake, he finally cornered his quarry and was about to jump her, when George Kennedy (a cop, of course) appeared, threw the attacker to the ground, and shot him dead. Consoling the shaking woman, Kennedy said: "I don't know what it is. Earthquakes bring out the worst in some guys."

The other line was much more unusual and exotic so it presented a much greater challenge. It was spoken by Nigel Bruce as Dr. Watson in one of the Sherlock Holmes movies of the 1940s when Watson was attempting to impress a couple on a ship who evidently were not familiar with Holmes's exploits. "Haven't you heard of the giant rat of Sumatra?" asked Watson, referring to one of the great detective's most famous cases. "Haven't you heard of the giant rat of Sumatra?"

Years, decades, passed, and I never came close to a moment when I might work in that line. The degree of difficulty was steep. There were so many elements to the

Watson remark. If one heard an opening for the rat, there would still be the matter of its size. If the rat and the size were there, one still had to contend with Sumatra. Above these concerns stood the context. In order to make the question really fit a situation, the opening had to allow for an attitude of superior surprise. "Haven't you heard of the giant rat of Sumatra?" Implying: "Who has not?"

In the late 1970s, I was writing for *The Washington Post,* and I had all but given up on my quest. In all those intervening years not a single conversation had come remotely close to offering me my longed-for opportunity. Then, one day, some friends and I went out to lunch, and it happened to be the fiftieth anniversary of the creation of Mickey Mouse. There was some chatter at the table about Mickey, to which I had been paying scant attention—how much he had contributed to American culture. The usual harmless claptrap. Suddenly, one of the guys sat up with a quizzical look and asked, "Has there ever been a bigger rodent?"

{ column in *The Washington Post* }

Flower Children

Their heads are bowed at their desks like the flowers I have given them. This is an in-class writing assignment: Write a page on what the flower smells like. It is an exercise in stream of consciousness for my students at the Southampton campus of Stony Brook University. The school is small and unadorned, spread out on a rise overlooking a bay. It is about to come into flowers of its own in the reluctant spring thaw.

Write what it smells like. Go into the past. Follow your nose. This is what you will do as writers. You will plunder the past to explain the present and make the present more intense. Think of stream of consciousness as a detour off the path of the narrative. Go where it takes you, and when you get back, the main road will have changed. So they sniff, dream into the pictures their minds unearth, and write. A boy's hand is fixed to his forehead, covering one eye. A girl touches her lips with her pencil. They are all very still, separated from one another and from the classroom and the cold sun streaking in.

While they do their exercise, they become mine. Write what they look like: fifteen young people in jeans, sweatshirts, and sweaters, bodies hooked over a white sheet of paper, pursuing memories, dressing them up, and watching to ascertain that their hands are following their minds' instructions. The flower is laid aside on the desk, its work done. The students are off now like hounds. They follow the scent to funerals, weddings, proms. One girl will remember lying in the night grass under a blue moon with her little sister. Another will recall a last dance with a midshipman in navy whites. A boy will alter the scent to that of lilacs, and swoop back to a childhood Eden near his father's rectory.

This is where education becomes private. This is the nub of it. It is out of sync with the conventional images of education in America. Write about those images: the teacher is a pale, bloodless deacon, drained by unsatisfied longings, preposterous, out of things. She is the withered maiden, he is Ichabod Crane, humiliated to death by the village nitwit. The only way he gains respect is to become Glenn Ford in *Blackboard Jungle* and beat up the classroom hoods. There are exceptions like *Mr. Holland's Opus*. But the rule is Arnold in *Kindergarten Cop*.

For their part, students are depicted as at their most alive when they have as little to do with school as possible. Huck and Holden light out for their respective territories. Ferris Bueller is the god of glorious truancy. Or make an *Animal House,* and trash the joint.

School is anticreativity, antifreedom, anti-American—an attitude only logically contradicted by a society that insists on higher education for all and accreditations up to the eyeballs.

Not that this derision is difficult to understand. Education is a setup for ridicule. Old people stuck in place deliver old information to new people about to move up and out. The adamant versus the supple. The straitlaced versus the unlaced, over whom they exert a flimsy and temporary authority. Every classroom is an implicit smirk. Write what you feel. Okay, I feel I am going to sit here and accept what that tired old bird dishes out, and then I'm going out on the green to toss a Frisbee, flirt, chomp on an Egg McMuffin, *live*. I'm going to leave him in his own dust. Meanwhile, the teacher, ever desperate to exhibit vital signs, forages for inspirational material. How to convey that this stuff is essential? How to get across that what is not practically useful is more useful? They are salmon in springtime, and Professor Backward has one small porous net. To catch even one or two of these lovable fish. Is that worth a life, Mr. Chips? Fish and Chips?

I'm a half-time teacher, an amateur. It is the lifers who hold up the citadel, they who remain in the dusty stillness of the classrooms after the kids have tromped out. Amid the riot of *The Nutty Professor*, Eddie Murphy caught that look—all knowledgeable, all wistful, hopeless within his own superiority. Everything he makes vanishes except his monumental size. As he chalks one line of an equation on the blackboard, his belly erases the other line. He is a visual fat joke. But he has something to teach them. He takes them seriously.

"Take another minute to write. Then let's see what we've got."

They hunker down with their memories. Still so much to say. They have long ago left the smell of the flower behind and are taking the rapids. Their necks and shoulders are locked. Their hands are disembodied and skitter from left to right like the automatic returns on electric typewriters. Teaching is love, love teaching. One girl recalls her job selling roses at the side of the highway. Men stopped their cars to buy a bunch. She writes, "No one bought roses for me."

{ essay in *Time* magazine }

From the Memoir
Making Toast

Ordinarily, I don't believe in teachers letting students in on too much of their private lives. But I intentionally have told my students about my daughter Amy and our family situation. The students hear rumors, so my coming straight out with it clears the air and helps remove the possibility that they will get overly interested in me and not in the material. I do not wish to play the mysterious professor with the unspoken sorrow. Mainly, I'd like them to realize that we're all in the same boat. Everyone one of them has experienced one grief or another. I tell them about Amy only once.

I like my students this term, which makes for better classes—freer, more far-reaching discussions, and the possibility of surprises. One day, a thoughtful and quiet young woman in my modern poetry class was making a reference to the Metaphysicals. Out of the blue, she said, "I don't like John Donne." *Not like John Donne?* "He has nothing original to say," she said. I gave her the form-rescues-content argument, but she remained unpersuaded. "When you're older," I began. She gave me the don't-go-there look.

In early November, the class took up Anne Sexton. I had never thought much of Sexton, judging her to be in a minor league compared to such contemporaries as Sylvia Plath and Adrienne Rich. But the students and I were getting into "The Truth the Dead Know," and I liked the poem better than I'd remembered. "This line, 'In another country people die.' What does it mean?" I asked the class. A young man said, "It means that death happens to other people."

From the Book on Writing
Unless It Moves
the Human Heart

Wouldn't it be nice if you knew that your teaching had shape and unity, and that when a semester came to an end, you could see that every individual thing you said had organized itself into one overarching statement? But who knows? I liken teaching to writing, but the two enterprises diverge here, because any perception of the grand scheme depends on what the students pick up. You may intend a lovely consistency in what you're tossing them, but they still have to catch it. In fact, I do see unity to my teaching. What *they* see, I have no clue. It probably doesn't matter if they accept the parts without the whole. A few things are learned, and my wish for more may be plain vanity.

"You know what I hate about writing," says Suzanne. "It makes me crabby."

"Crabbier," her husband George corrects her.

"I get into something I'm writing," she says, "and I lose patience with family, friends, and, of course, *him*."

"You haven't begun to know crabbiness in writers." I tell her about the time Faulkner sent the manuscript of *Absalom, Absalom* to his editor. The editor was on vacation, so the manuscript was read by an assistant, who returned it, complaining that Faulkner's sentences were too long, his plot murky, and the whole thing a mess. Faulkner fired back a five-word telegram: "Who the hell are you?"

We are having drinks before our reunion dinner at

Robert's restaurant in Water Mill. It is late February 2010. I didn't have to inveigle Robert. Good guy that he is, he offered his place to the class, and we jumped. Our final meeting of the semester last May had begun with a lofty discussion of their artistic aims, and soon disintegrated into plans for their summer vacations. There is nothing like the light on eastern Long Island in late spring. By the time class ended, we all were stealing glances at the bright windows and hearing the ocean in our daydreams.

Now, still winter, patches of snow cling to the ground around Robert's. The restaurant occupies a handsome yellow-shingled house on the south side of Montauk Highway, which cuts through the center of Water Mill, between Southampton and Bridgehampton. The town has a windmill on its green. A stagecoach stop in the 1670s, Robert's retains an antique country feel, with pocket windows, candlestick wall lights, little sand-colored lampshades, wide-plank floors, dark beams on the ceiling both bearing and decorative, two fireplaces, and a large, wide, gleaming wood bar. The dining area is an L-shaped room, with a dozen tables, and a private room with an open entrance is framed by more beams. Here Robert's staff has set up a round table for the twelve of us. Only Nina couldn't make the dinner. Excited to see one another after a year, the students talk nonstop as soon as they take their seats, occasionally acknowledging that I am here too.

"How's the book about us coming?" asks Diana, who is all dressed up tonight in black slacks and a black sweater. We are seated at the round table, chatting before dinner.

"Oh, I've chucked the book. The characters were too flat—boring, if you know what I mean."

"You better treat us right," says Sven, a very good writer, and a bruiser.

"What are you going to do, beat me up?" I smile my old man's smile.

"Has it been hard to write?" asks Veronique.

"It would have been, if I had used things you actually said. But the stuff I made up is so much better—brighter, funnier—than could ever have come out of your mouths."

"So you're finished?" asks Jasmine. "I guess it's time to call the lawyer."

"Class action," says George.

"I hope you included all the things you learned from us," says Jasmine. "Teachers always say how much they learn from their students."

"They must have different students."

"Did you ever feel you couldn't do the book?" Kristie asks. She too is dressed for the party. All the women look aglow.

I tell them about a conversation last week, with my three-year-old grandson, James.

He looked at a bunch of papers on my bed. "What are you doing, Boppo?" he asked. "Writing a book about teaching people how to write."

"But people already know how to write," said James. "You don't need to teach them."

"To James!" says Inur, raising a toast. In the year since our last class, she has married a lawyer and lives in New York. After a day of appointments in the city, she made the two-and-a-half-hour drive to Robert's to be with us.

"Are you writing?" I ask her.

"I'm starting to write again," she says. "It's been a while. I don't have a job now, so there's plenty of free time."

She has her right arm in a cast, from a fall on the ice. Suzanne helps her cut her food. When Inur entered the room, we all laughed because Veronique had arrived a short while earlier with her *left* arm in a cast. She dislocated her shoulder in a fall down a flight of stairs. Veronique announces to the group that she's in love. "At forty-four! At last!" Inspecting her arm, George croons, "Falling in love with love."

Jasmine is looking for work in publishing and has a nibble from a Long Island magazine. She is writing "every single day," she tells me. I forgot how fresh and sweet her face is. Her hair is done up in bright ringlets.

We raise our glasses to Robert. His play, *Alternate Spaces,* will be put on at the Southampton Arts Festival this spring, as will a play by Diana. Diana has also begun to teach Stony Brook undergraduates.

"I'm writing plays. I'm writing everything," says Diana. "Wonder where I got that idea." (I teach a course called "Writing Everything.")

"Think you want to be a playwright?"

"I never want to do just one genre," she says. "And I don't want a real job. I don't want to be real."

"How come the course didn't cover playwriting?" asks George.

"There wasn't enough time. And I don't know much about plays."

"You write them," says Suzanne.

"That's what I mean." I taught a playwriting class some years ago, which went okay but nothing great. One thing worked. I gave my students an exercise that emerged from a conversation I'd had with Wendy Wasserstein. Wendy had said that she knew she was really into the writing of a play when she had created a third character. I had my students set up a situation consisting of two people. Once they had done that, I asked them to introduce a third character, to see how things were shaken up. We also discussed the rhythm of the action of a play, and the odd fact that in dialogue, no one's really speaking to anyone else. But that was about it. Most of the class was spent with the students simply enjoying one another's plays.

"How's teaching going, Kristie?" She teaches a "developmental" class at her community college. Ana, something of a cultured snob, is amused by the euphemism. Kristie says she has to go over assignments again and again, "and still they come up after class and say, 'What's the assignment?'" It's clear that she is very good for the students by whom she is less exasperated than tickled. "There's a navy vet in my class. He sat next to a girl who said not a word to him for the whole semester. On the last day, she looked at him. 'You're like older, right?' she said. 'And you're in the army or something? You do drugs?'"

Kristie and Diana trade funny teaching stories. Ana tells of having a dinner party where, scared to death, she found herself preparing dinner for the greatest cook in Europe. George, who is built like a 300-pound roast, tells us he used to be a food critic. "I weighed a hundred and ninety pounds before that." He laughs. "The job did me in."

"Out," says Suzanne.

Like Diana, Sven is writing in new and different forms. "I used to think I was a short story writer," he says. "Now I'm finding stories the hardest to do."

Donna has sent out four stories in the past year, all rejected, though she received an encouraging note from the editor of *National Geographic*. "Is that good?"

"You bet it is." I start to tell her not to be discouraged by the rejections. But one look tells me that's unnecessary. She's hooked. They all are.

"May we talk about stuff you never let us talk about in class?" says Sven.

"Like what?"

"Things writers do other than write."

"Like drink?"

"Like readings. The thought of giving a public reading of anything I wrote scares me to death," says Veronique.

"I love going to poetry readings," says Suzanne. George and others nod. "Poets are so crazy. You can see it in their faces. It's great."

"I think they're sexy," says Inur. "Not like prose writers." She indicates me.

"Do you think poetry readings are better than readings by novelists and essayists?" Jasmine asks me.

"Probably, if the poet is a good reader, like Billy Collins, or Dylan Thomas. Robert Lowell was a terrible reader, and if you've ever heard recordings of the vaguely British, dry-as-dust voice of T. S. Eliot, you'll wonder what happened to his hometown of St. Louis."

"Poetry readers are easier to listen to," says Ana. "Because the readings come in short bites."

"Did you ever hear Billy's joke about imagining Dante at the lectern as he was about to give a reading? Dante says, 'I'll just read three poems.'" I tell them to be careful about reading their work too well, that mistakes can be covered up by hypnotic voices. "Your silent, private reader won't cut you as much slack. You should have fun with readings, poetry or prose, because the audience can't really understand everything it hears. You might as well make the most of it. Years ago I saw a cartoon in a magazine, in two frames. A writer bends over his book at a reading. He looks up at the audience and says, 'Oh. You mean *aloud!*'"

"I'd like to talk about the writing life," says Diana.

I am about to say, "What life?" but I hold my tongue.

"You mean things about the way writers live? I have no idea how you should live."

"Yeah," says Donna. "Let's get down to all that stuff you hate to talk about—editors, publishers, advances, agents. Fame!"

"Let's get real," says Diana.

"A few minutes ago you said that you didn't want to be real."

"Come on," says Jasmine. "We're not in a classroom now. You won't lose your virtue."

"Everyone sinks to the lowest level at Robert's," says Robert, raising his shot glass. "It's a regular joint."

"All right." I sigh dramatically. "You want to know about agents? I cannot tell you how to get one. My agent, Gloria Loomis, has been with me for thirty-four years. When I started out writing for *The New Republic,* Gloria read an essay I wrote and called to ask if she could represent me. I was so flattered, I think I said 'Huh?' or 'Wow!'—something sophisticated like that."

"So we should all get jobs at *The New Republic* and wait to be discovered?" says Diana.

"Yes."

"Why does everyone look down on agents?" says Inur.

"Because they are indispensable, like dentists and lawyers. And they're subject to the same jokes. They deal with all the things you don't want to touch."

"Money!" says Donna.

"Money."

"What about editors?" asks Ana.

"You have to be lucky, and I've been lucky there, too. There are very few real editors these days. Most people who call themselves editors merely acquire books or authors. They don't get into the texts, and by that I do not mean line-editing or copyediting. Great editors determine what it is you want to say—"

"What is this *about*?" says Veronique.

"Exactly. Great editors become their authors. They question what you have written the way you would yourself, had you come up with the question. It's a weird process for a writer. First you resist a correction or a suggestion, thinking, 'That can't possibly be right.' Then you realize that your editor has seen your intentions more completely than you have. They will tell you what you meant to say. They will point out what's missing, or whether you need a new direction, or that you ought to go further in the direction you've chosen."

"Some writers say they don't need an editor," says Sven.

"Not the good ones. In the very least, an editor saves your ass. I've never known a good writer who did not profit from the hand of a first-rate editor. Sven? You have any more questions?"

"This may sound funny," he says. "But is there a particular kind of place a writer should live? Is one location or another better for one's work?"

"It doesn't matter where you live. Country, city, suburb—all three have been home to great writers. It doesn't matter how much money you have, either, though try to live within the general vicinity of your means. You don't want money to drive your artistic decisions, and poverty will do that to you. Neither does it matter if you hold another job while you write, especially if you need to pay the heating bill. Chaucer was a civil servant, Keats and Joyce were medical students. Wallace Stevens an insurance man. Melville a customs inspector. Nathanael West was the night manager in a cheap hotel. Frank O'Hara worked at the ticket counter in the Museum of Modern Art. It is common practice to advise young writers to take jobs that have nothing to do with reading and writing, so as to create some space between the real world and the imagined."

"We've heard that a lot," says Inur.

"But being a book editor didn't get in T. S. Eliot's way. And writers such as Doctorow, Alice McDermott, and Ann Beattie continue to teach writing and literature. The trick is to find your place in the world—your town, your home, your room—which is usually achieved by hit-and-miss. After that, the trick is to recognize what you've got once you've got it, and not to let success or ambition lead you away from it. It took me thirty years to realize that where I wanted to be was in a lumpy white chair positioned at a forty-degree angle from a window looking out on a pine tree in front of my house."

"What about your friends?" asks Inur. "Should writers hang out with other writers?"

"Or we shall all hang separately," says George.

Many young writers seek the company of other young writers because they share a common world of gripes, celebrations, professional problems and interests, and because companionship lessens their loneliness. Dr. Johnson had his circle, Keats his. Both groups consisted of artistic folks such as Boswell, Joshua Reynolds, and Leigh Hunt. Hemingway chose a rougher crowd made up of boxers, big-game hunters, and Gertrude Stein. These little conventions are usually pictured in convivial situations, like weekly dinners in picturesque taverns. The participants are shown being witty and happy together, though I saw a black-and-white photo of Joseph Heller, James Jones, Truman Capote, and others drinking together in a Hamptons dive, each seemingly competing for the title of "Grimmest

Face in America." Yet for Johnson, Keats, Hemingway, or any first-rate writer, the idea of clubby companionship is nearly always a pretense. History's more amiable writers, such as Oliver Goldsmith and Charles Lamb, were anomalies. And the most famous American circle, the Algonquin Round Table in New York, had no first-rate writers at all.

"At the outset of your careers, you will probably enjoy the company of others for a while, up to the point that you know for certain what your life's subject is, and your craftsmanship has risen to meet it. Then you will notice that you are increasingly disinclined to be in contact with your old friends, even the most beloved. Your husband, wife, partner, whoever, will constitute all the social life you need, and surprisingly little of that. In the end, you will find yourself glorifying in that same solitude you sought to avoid at the start."

"Do you think our group could become a circle of writers?" asks Kristie.

"First become writers."

"Will we all turn out to be disagreeable old men like you?" asks Jasmine.

"If you're lucky."

"I think you're suggesting that we shouldn't get married or live with someone," says Kristie.

"Too late," says Suzanne, turning to George.

"What sort of person would want to live with a writer?" asks Veronique.

"A patient one."

"Should a writer marry another writer?" asks Jasmine.

"A patient one"—and before they tell me that my wife must be very patient, I suggest we order dinner.

For three hours more we sit and enjoy one another's company. We drink. We overeat—lobster bisque, polenta, lamb, salmon, rib eye. The talk glides from Shakespeare and Jane Austen to Steven Seagal and Nicolas Cage and Tiger Woods, and a guy who delivered pot-laced brownies to the office where Inur once worked. I sit back and listen. After two shots of Jameson's neat, everything can look lovable, but cold sober I would love this group, especially for their affection for one another. Kristie asked me if they might become a literary circle. They are something better—a circle of friends.

Diana looks up at me, sensing we are about to call it a night. "Is there anything you haven't told us?" she asks. "Last chance."

"That's hard to imagine," says Suzanne to the others. "He's talked too much. Yak yak yak."

"Well, there is something I might have mentioned, but it's difficult, so I didn't think you were up to understanding it. Anyway, it's too late now." I get my coat, and move toward the door, accompanied by a chorus of boos. We hug, and we part.

Form Rescues Content

Cloud-ghosts pass along the skull of the sky. Two gulls wheel by together. A single-engine plane drones eastward. Purposeful little bugger, it makes a beeline. The sun is a blur, a slowing pulse. The water looks shellacked. I poke about at the shore, where the creek has worn lines in the rocks. The rocks bear evidence of the creek. If the creek should dry up, the rocks would know it existed. The moon slides out of sight, in its secret night. I am contained in my boat. Form rescues content.

{ from the memoir *Kayak Morning* }

If It's Just a Teeny-Weeny Bit Wrong—Destroy It

Advocates of writing with word processors tend to promote the practice by pointing out how easy it is to make corrections. In the flick of a key one may transpose paragraph 19 for paragraph 37, chapter 5 may become chapter 20, and so forth. People tout these "conveniences" to illustrate the facility with which a manuscript may be repaired and how much time can be saved.

Nonsense. Time has actually been lost. In writing, if one thing is wrong, the whole thing is wrong. And the smaller the wrong thing appears, the larger the overall error. Writers spend months wondering what to do with the third sentence from the bottom of paragraph 4, page 307, when they would be better off gently picking up the entire manuscript and walking ceremoniously to the trash can.

What is true for writing is true for other things. If an outfit is a little wrong, it is all wrong. If a friendship is a little wrong, it is all wrong. Think of little errors not as aberrations but as cautionary symbols, representative of the whole.

I realize that this rule will deprive you of the pleasure of pretending that a few minimalistic repairs are all that your life requires. That, of course, is the purpose of these rules—to take away your fun.

{ from the instruction book *Rules for Aging* }

As Good as It Gets

When I was thirteen or so, I watched a movie in which a young writer (played by Frank Sinatra?) and his girlfriend go to an Italian restaurant to celebrate the acceptance of his first short story. The restaurant's owner is celebrating too, as are all the people sitting at the other tables, which are covered with checkerboard tablecloths and lit by candles dripping wax. Everyone wishes the writer well, no one more than I, who tried to foresee such a moment when I, too, would become a writer. The acceptance of the story. The cheers. The girl and the life of my dreams.

Most films about the writing life are more accurate, because writers write them. And rarely is the writer shown as successful, triumphant or—are you kidding?—happy. This subject comes to mind at the time of the Academy Awards, which has no category for Best Film About a Writer, so, unbidden, I'm going to nominate three. It wasn't easy whittling down the number. So many runners-up: *The Front,* about Hollywood blacklisting, is a terrific picture written by a terrific screenwriter, Walter Bernstein. Woody Allen's *Deconstructing Harry* seems merely clever, but its ingenuity glides into something interesting when the writer literally slips out of focus, just like his fictional character. More than clever, too, is *Stranger Than Fiction,* in which the life of an IRS auditor is narrated by a novelist who plans to kill him off. Only when human kindness changes her mind does the story ring false.

Some might suggest other contenders: *Shadowlands; Barton Fink; Adaptation;* the creepy *Secret Window;* the scary *Misery;* and *Limitless,* starring Bradley Cooper, one of this year's Oscar nominees, as a writer who takes a drug that allows him to use his whole brain, as opposed to those of us who use everyone else's.

Writers like watching movies about themselves. It gives us something to do. My doctor father used to scoff at movies about doctors because he was always finding fault with some diagnosis or treatment. I don't know how cops or lawyers feel about their portrayals. Politicians are usually shown as corruptible. Teachers as sad. Writers, with the exception of that movie I saw as a kid, are variously crazy (Jack Nicholson in *The Shining*), reckless (Michael Douglas in *Wonder Boys*), cranky (Van Johnson in *23 Paces to Baker Street*), self-destructive (Ray Milland in *The Lost Weekend*), without principle (William Holden in *Sunset Boulevard*) and/or flailing (Paul Giamatti in *Sideways*). Nothing to argue with, really.

What we are not shown doing in movies is writing. Composers are shown composing because we can listen to their flights of fancy on the soundtrack. Painters are shown painting, because one can actually see art in progress. Kirk Douglas did some very good van Gogh impressions. Ed Harris went so hog wild in *Pollock,* one was tempted to go out and buy an original Harris. But writers are rarely shown laboring at the craft unless you count Nicholson's "all work and no play." I suppose there's nothing visually dramatic in what we do, though we can get quite worked up about crumpling little balls of paper and tossing them on the floor.

I ought to say I have excluded from consideration films about journalists as writers, because journalists are employed and moored to institutions; thus, while depressed and self-hating, they are less so than untethered writers, try as they might. They have company.

Still there are some wonderful films about journalists in pursuit of a story: *Citizen Kane, The Year of Living Dangerously, It Happened One Night, Foreign Correspondent.*

Excluded, too, are films about famous writers, which are clunky in the way films about famous people are clunky in general. ("Billy? May I introduce my two good friends, Gerard Manley Hopkins and Sarah Orne Jewett?") My three chosen films are all good ones, both in themselves, and because they show us writers for what we are (besides unhappy): misfits who occasionally act nobly and honorably in life, yet are also more than a little afraid of it. Before the tension becomes unbearable, the winners are:

The Third Man (1949) is about corruption and divided loyalty, but also about a writer who knows who he is and knows his limits. Holly Martins, an author of Westerns, comes to postwar Vienna to find his friend, Harry Lime. He learns that Lime was reportedly killed in a hit-and-run, but begins to suspect otherwise. Sinister people chase him. One wonderful scene has him taking refuge at a literary society meeting, to which he was invited because the members heard he was a writer. He's asked if he was influenced by Thomas Gray. He tells them the Grey he was influenced by was Zane, and he has no opinion of "Mr. James Joyce." finding that Lime has faked his own death to avoid arrest as a black-marketeering murderer of sick children, the writer of westerns must don his white hat and turn on his friend. He is true to his genre. In the end, he shoots the bad guy, not to the music of a guitar but to the strum of a zither.

Starting Out in the Evening may be the only film about an important writer that persuades you he's important. Leonard Schiller (Frank Langella), forgotten by readers, is pursued by Heather Wolfe (Lauren Ambrose), who is doing her master's thesis on his work, so, in a way, this is a horror film. The beauty of it comes from Leonard, a widower, who is reserved, formal, and ailing. Despite readers' neglect, he continues to write, taking art as seriously as it deserves to be taken. Reluctantly, he agrees to weekly meetings with Heather, who is smart but shallow, and overly interested in Leonard's personal life. They sleep together once, but it is beside the point. The point is Leonard, the pure, single-minded writer. We can't take our eyes off him.

Breakfast at Tiffany's, Blake Edwards's near-perfect film version of Truman Capote's novella, centers on the fragile eccentric, Holly Golightly (Audrey Hepburn), but the writer, Paul Varjak (George Peppard), bears as much watching. Holly wants out of her life; Paul wants into his. He is a kept man who has not published anything since a critically successful book of short stories. One telling scene shows the apparently scatterbrained Holly hunkered down over Paul's book in the New York Public Library.

Silently, she is drawn to his words, as are we to her. After failing to win a life with some wealthy jerk from Brazil, and having learned of the death of her cherished brother, Holly is in despair. But Paul, because he falls in love with her, discovers himself as a man and as an artist. He finds authentic love, which rescues them both.

Nominees aside, my sentimental favorite portrait of a writer occurs in a film not as good in itself as any of the above, but one that offers writers the incomparable satisfaction of getting a piece of work right. *Bullets Over Broadway* stars the can-do-no-wrong Dianne Wiest as the deliciously manipulative actress Helen Sinclair, and the can-do-nothing-unappealing John Cusack as the terrible playwright David Shayne. But for the writers in the audience, the hero is Chazz Palminteri, who plays a gangster named Cheech. Shayne can't write a lick. But Cheech is a natural, his writerly instincts so dead on, one laughs aloud in sublime appreciation of every improvement he makes in Shayne's play.

What's more, he's never tentative. And while he buys it in the end, as gangsters must, he has made every writer who sees this film happy to be doing what we're doing. Happy to be who we are. Happy. Do you hear?

{ essay in *The New York Times Book Review* }

From the Memoir
The Boy Detective

And in case you were wondering—because *I* certainly was wondering—this may be as good a place as any to talk about Wallace Stevens's "Tea at the Palaz of Hoon." Not that you ever mentioned the poem. And not that I am at all sure I have the meaning down cold myself. But in spite of all the ellipses in that poem (four-dotters, if there were such a thing), it seems clear that the poem is about the created self. And a boy detective knows something about the created self.

So the idea, I think, is that we live with real people and real events, yet we feel like fictions traveling among them. This is because, while the externalities of our lives remain stable, even adamant, we function in a continual state of self-creation, malleable, fluent.

When the Hoon poem states at the end, "I was the world in which I walked," it means that the poet influences the conscious life about him by making an imaginative construction of himself. And that this self, the detective or the writer, though he moves about in "the loneliest air," is hardly lonely. Indeed, he celebrates (privately), because he finds himself, as a result of his illimitable walks, "more truly and more strange."

Yet this is where the detective's and the writer's view of things becomes a bit tricky, because the world the detective observes, while not imagined, has all the thrills of an imagined construct. Holmes means it in "A Case of Identity," when he tells Watson that "life is infinitely stranger than anything which the mind of man could invent." And just when we find ourselves agreeing with Holmes, and rooting for nonfiction over fiction, it comes to us that Holmes is himself a fictional creation. So Conan Doyle is playing us here, but also making a point. Holmes, not real, instructs Watson, not real, in the wonders of reality. The wonder is Holmes himself, the fictional detective in pursuit of a fictional crime that he creates the fiction of solving. Truth is, nothing ever is solved in a Sherlock Holmes story because it never happened. If life is "infinitely stranger" than fiction, how could one ever solve its mysteries?

In any case—and frankly, you can get a fine old headache trying to work out "Tea at the Palaz of Hoon," the very title of which suggests that Stevens intended to give us a headache—the poem is happy. I was the world in which I walked. And though I moved through the loneliest air, hardly was I lonely. No less was I myself. I was more myself. My boy detective. My self-created self. Happy. Fairly happy. In case you were wondering.

Aubade

Inseparable from the dark dawn, this white chair, sweat-stained at the top of the back cushion, and the ink scratches on its arms. This yellow pad. This Bic without its top.

This silence and these words that remain silent yet push and elbow each other out of the way like mimes vying for attention.

These dreams that go forward and back, past scoundrels and geese in great flights and the outrages of history, which, since they are dreams, become birds, then baseballs, then blues numbers and my dad in his kitchen, singing show tunes in his slippers.

This morning, this life. One could die of happiness.

{ from the essay collection *Anything Can Happen* }

From the Novel
Thomas Murphy

Whereas today I walk the city in my head dug in like a plough, mired. I hate these writerly moods, their selfishness, grotesque. Around me march my beautiful New Yorkers with their cowled faces, flayed by the wind, fresh from their vile mills. They hear the drumming of real graves, while I, fancy me, indulge myself in a pastime. Greenberg would have ribbed me without mercy. Oona too. Me too. Snap out of it, Murph. In a day, an hour, I will be on a high again, thrilled to the bone to be permitted life and poetry, thrilled to have Máire with me and to be able to read William to sleep twice a week—while they, my beautiful New Yorkers, have not the luxury of mood swings. Or moods at all, for Chrissake. Courage with resignation. That's their bloody mood. One mood forever. How I adore them, though I would not tell them so, lest I sound patronizing, as if I were accepting them, when the opposite is true. They accept me. Me, the freakish exception to the rules of their existence. What one must do as a poet, before placing the right words in the right order, before wandering lonely as a cloud or summoning a second coming, is to recognize the precious gift of one's perch, and then walk with one's fellow citizens and feel their powerless power. I push my body into my beautiful New Yorkers, and vanish with them in the brown, humiliating earth.

Dream up, not down. Up. Tyrants dream down, businessmen dream laterally, poets dream up. That's how you can remember it. Dream up.

From the Memoir
Making Toast

Long ago, I abandoned all hope that I would ever learn anything new again—too few remaining brain cells. Now, thanks to the reading I do with my grandson Sammy before bedtime, I teem with information about trucks, boats, planes, cranes, and drilling equipment. Last night, after Sammy and I had discussed the comparative strengths of stabilizers and forklifts, I lay down for a while with my granddaughter Jessie. My wife, Ginny, had finished two chapters of *James and the Giant Peach* with her, and my son-in-law, Harris, was in with my grandson James. Jessie was ready to pick up another book—*Harold and the Purple Crayon*—which she read to me.

"Harold creates his own world," said Jessie. "Like writers," I said. Jessie has variously wanted to be a writer, a doctor, a fashion model, and an orchestra conductor. "If you decide to become a writer, Jess, you can create anything you like—friends, princesses, monsters."

"New worlds, too," she said.

"New planets." I said. "Harold not only creates his own world, he lives in it. That's like writers, too. Another way of saying it is that writers *inhabit* their own worlds."

Jessie said, "*Inhabit*. Let's make that tomorrow's Word for the Morning."

I said, "Let's *do* that."

We continued talking about all that a writer can create, like Harold. I said that sometimes, when one creates, one does not find what one is looking for right away, and so must keep creating until it appears. He may even have created it before, but he lost it, and now he must imagine it again. "Like Harold's window," said Jessie. With his crayon, Harold draws first one window, then two, and then an entire city of windows in an effort to discover the window he lost. "Exactly like Harold's window," I said.

Things Invisible to See

A couple of years ago, in an essay in *The New Yorker,* the critic and writer Kathryn Schulz pointed out that we cannot see most of the things that rule our lives. Magnetic fields, electric currents, the force of gravity all work unseen, as do our interior arbiters of thoughts, inclinations, passions, psyches, tastes, moods, morals, and—if one believes in them—souls. The invisible world governs the visible like a hidden nation-state.

The same is true of writing. You come up with an image, phrase, or sentence. Your head snaps back, and you say to yourself, Where did *that* come from?! I'm not talking about automatic writing, though that may be part of it. I mean the entire range of invisible forces that produce and affect the work. There are things the writer sees that the reader does not; things the reader sees that the writer does not; and things neither of us ever sees. These, the most entrancing of the lot, have a power of their own. Like the ghost of Jacob Marley, they lead to unimagined, sometimes frightful yet fruitful destinations.

What the writer sees and keeps from the reader is the simplest of the three, because it deals mainly with craft. The planting of clues in poetry or prose, for instance. If we're doing our job, readers have no idea that what they have just read—a name, a place—will be picked up later in the piece, heaving with meaning. The clue is invisible as a clue. In a sense, the whole novel, play, essay, or poem is invisible. The reader does not recognize the work (what writers call "work") that goes into the choices we fiddle with and blunder into before landing on the right ones. That's as it should be. "If it does not seem a moment's thought," said Yeats, "our stitching and unstitching has been naught."

Neither does the reader ever see the first draft, or the second, or the nineteenth. That the writer knows and recalls these drafts, even if dimly, has an invisible effect of its own. As a stanza or a character becomes better wrought, the writer more fully comprehends her or his intentions with the piece. An early draft is the child that becomes the man, who is more deeply understood for the author having witnessed the book's strange, meandering growth every step of the way. Fitzgerald's first stabs at *The Great Gatsby* had Tom, Daisy, Jordan, and Gatsby going to a baseball game, a narrator named Dudley (or Dud), and two green lights at the end of Daisy's dock. Hovering discarded phantoms.

And the writer knows what has happened in a story before the story begins. All short stories are over before we read the first line. The story itself constitutes the key moment, the consequence of the invisible story that preceded it. Salinger had to know all about Seymour Glass before Seymour wound up in Florida, when we meet him in "A Perfect Day for Bananafish." By that time, everything is too late.

What does the reader see that's invisible to the writer? Mainly, his or her own life. You write a book and send it into space. You have no idea where it lands—what effects it will have on a reader, who is invisible to you. There is that lovely moment for a writer when someone will say, Your book changed my life. (Lovely, that is, unless it changed it for the worse.) Writers do not see their readers, who remain a secret, with secret lives. Our transaction is unseen. We only hope that what we do is so generally true that those who read us will embrace our efforts as part of their stories. We write to an invisible world on which we depend. If you happen to recognize yourself in someone or something we create, that's all good. But the writer will never know that, or you. You are Harvey, our invisible, six-foot (we hope, gentle), big-eared friend.

But the greatest, and in some ways, the most satisfying invisibility is that world which neither writer nor reader will ever see, and yet knows exists. Jules Feiffer tells the story of starting his cartoons for the *Village Voice*. Before his first strip came out, his mother—who terrified and tyrannized Jules—warned him that if there were a terrifying, tyrannizing woman in the strip, it better not look like her! Confident that his drawing looked nothing like his mother, Jules assured her she was safe. When the strip came out, Jules writes in his memoir, he stared at it. There was his mother.

Who knows where anything comes from in writing? Whatever the source, most writers feel some inspirational push or tug connected with the work. And the inspirations have mysterious maps. Many a writer has started out certain of a particular direction only to change course midway, as though a ghost's hand took the tiller.

I am not unaware that my writing has improved in the nine years since our daughter's death. My work is sharper now, and more careful. Happily would I trade all the books I've written in those nine years for one moment with my daughter Amy alive, but since that bargain is impossible, I write to fill the void her death created. And something else: Since I believe it was Amy's death that led me to write more seriously, she lives with me invisible. I write to see her.

{ essay in *The New York Times Book Review* }

From the Memoir
Kayak Morning

Only literary jerks like me think of *Moby-Dick* in Starbucks. Seeing the world through a book darkly. I'm not sure it's good for you. A group of us English graduate students used to eat in a diner, where we always were served by the same waitress. She was tall, with black hair and a lyrical voice. One day she asked what we were studying, and we told her the Romantics. "Oh," she said, "I'd love to read that!" So we gave her a book of Byron. She returned it a day later. "I don't get it," she said. "Where's the romance?"

And yet there was Leon Wieseltier, shortly after my daughter, Amy, died, giving me an annotated version of Wordsworth's "The Excursion." I'd skimmed the poem in graduate school but never attached it to my life. For a year I let the heavy volume sit on my desk, knowing Leon would not have given it to me had he not determined that it would matter. Leon reads the soul. And then one afternoon, when the Bethesda house was quiet and the children still at school, and I alone, I opened the poem to Book Four, taking in the lines: "One in whom persuasion and belief / Had ripened into faith, and faith became a passionate intuition." I may have been without religion, but I used to have faith. Now I was without faith and belief and persuasion, too, and thus without passion. I read the lines and saw where I was.

Keats wrote of Fanny Brawne, "Everything that reminds me of her goes through me like a spear."

All I have to keep me afloat, all I have ever had, is writing. In 2008, I wrote an essay in *The New Yorker* about our family after Amy's death. A year later, I expanded the piece into a book, *Making Toast*. In it, I tried to suggest that the best one can do in a situation such as ours is to get on with it. I believe that still. What I failed to calculate is the pain that increases even as one gets on with it. The response to the book indicated how many others have experienced similar losses and feelings. I have received nearly a thousand letters from people telling me their stories and wishing our family well. The letters keep coming. Everybody grieves.

A woman approached me on the street in New York. I had never seen her before.

"I read your book," she said.

"I'm sorry for your loss," I said.

Be kind, for everyone you meet is carrying a great burden.

—Attributed to Philo

From the Unpublished Novel Young Murph

Death means losing, in every way. Does it not? You lose your own life. You lose others. A guy dies. The doctor says, We lost him. Life means losing, too. You lose time, opportunity, poems. You lose poems. An Englishman named Empson wrote that. The dead fisherman was lost and remains lost. And the world goes on in a tacit, unconscious dirge in his honor. Fearing to lose all, Joyce's Stephen Dedalus wrote his way out of sorrow. Does the act of writing hold back the losses, cut the losses? Or does it make one more aware of what is being lost, of the process of loss itself? As soon as the thought becomes the word, you lose it. As soon as the word hits the paper, you lose it. Small wonder there is a feeling of dissatisfaction when one finishes a poem. Fearing to lose all, you lose all anyway.

Dead Bird

It's egocentric, I know. But writers wonder if our work will last, because immortality, or our small version of it, does not depend solely on what we write, but rather on strangers of the future, who will either take us or leave us. Think of it. Without T. S. Eliot's act of literary resurrection, John Donne would have disappeared. Poof. Not even a thing invisible to see. It's possible that Shakespeare would have vanished without a trace, had not the eighteenth century revived him. In our words we leave evidence that we lived, but words are so light and fragile they can disintegrate at the touch.

Yesterday afternoon, I heard a thud coming from the area of the kitchen. When I went to look, a dead bird was lying on the deck outside my glass door. The door had killed the bird, which must have mistaken the glass for open air in the bright sunshine. The bird's body left an imprint on the glass, vague and lacy, like a smoke ring from a cigarette. The imprint made a nearly complete circle, except for a smudge at the top where the bird's head may have hit. I don't know about birds. This one was colorful—green, orange, and brown—like a mallard duck, though it was smaller than a duck. The little guy lay on its back on the deck, and when I picked it up with a paper towel, to put it in a plastic bag, the bird was heavier than I'd anticipated. It had heft and substance. Only when I had tossed it in the trash, and returned to my door, did I notice the imprint on the glass. It was there yesterday, and it is here this morning. I will wipe the door clean eventually, but not today. The smoky white ring is all that's left of the bird.

{ essay in *The Kenyon Review* }

Love Song

If those pushy mothers of the Plaza de Mayo, years ago in Argentina, didn't go away no matter how the *policia* shoved them around; if they continued to walk up and down in front of the presidential Pink House carrying photographs on placards and holding snapshots between their index fingers and their thumbs; if they insisted day after day, sunshine or rain, that their children did indeed exist in spite of the fact that they had been "disappeared" by the thugs of the military government, proving by their dogged persistence that there was no such thing as a *desaparecido* or that nothing beloved could vanish just like that . . . why would you think that books could disappear?

{ from the extended essay *The Book of Love* }

The Writer as Detective

Since nine-year-olds didn't wear suit jackets, I had to carry my revolver in a jury-rigged shoulder holster under my polo shirt. The look was that of a kid who had just snitched a mango from a fruit stand and was unsuccessfully trying to conceal it. The cap gun was cold against my chest, yet I maintained a grim, professional demeanor, lest my suspects spot any weakness and get the upper hand. I trailed them among the secret stores and wholesale houses of New York's East Twenties, a nei-ther-here-nor-there area north of Gramercy Park, where I lived. The place looked innocuous enough, but was clearly teeming with crime. The businessmen I shadowed also looked harmless, to anyone but me. I trailed them at short distances, making it easy for them to notice me, because if the killer did not know he was being followed, no one else would either. I saw myself as acting simultaneously in real time and in a film noir, so I was both tracking my quarry and watching myself do it.

For his part, the killer, sensing danger, would turn around from time to time, confused and annoyed at being pursued by a kid with a mango in his shirt.

My reasons for taking up the detective business were the usual ones. I was bored by my parents, my school, my respectable neighborhood, and by childhood. I was bored to death by childhood. The more fundamental rea-son, however, was that I loved living in a mystery. Thus, though I hardly knew it at the time, I was becoming a writer, or to be more accurate, I was thinking and feeling like a writer. E. L. Doctorow likened his writing process to driving at night, when you can see no farther than where the headlights illuminate (a film noir image if ever there was one). This method will take you only so far, since at some point in the act of writing, the ending will crook its siren finger and beckon you to leap into the light. Yet it is the darkness where the thrills occur, and the lurid pictures, and the base thoughts, and the strange words to describe them, and you giddily are lost among unseen and unheard-of things. Writers answer questions no one asks. Others tell what they know. Writers imagine what they know.

So we move about our odd trade, looking as weird as kid detectives on the street, pursuing criminals of our own manufacture, and making nuisances of ourselves. We trust the dark as others trust the light, not to solve our mysteries but to hold us in their thrall. When we approach something that smacks of a solution, it is disappointing. We try to hold it off. At the end of *The Thin Man,* Nick Charles assembles his suspects at a dinner party before exposing the killer. He prattles on until Nora, impatient and frustrated, demands to know who did it. Nick says he doesn't know. He seems to be stalling. The mystery of *The Thin Man* is so delicious, who would want it solved?

In fact, Nick isn't stalling. He really doesn't know who the killer is until the killer reveals himself. Nick has simply made the revelation inevitable, after following enough shady people down enough grimy streets. As a writer, you create characters who act differently than you ever supposed, circumstances that change shape and direction, sentences that seem to emerge from a trance. Ideas occur to you that you never knew you had, opinions you never knew you held. Only reluctantly do you concede that the mystery must eventually get hold of itself and come to order. In a conversation recently, when I was making the commonplace complaints about religions, a friend remarked that without religions people might go mad from life's mysteries. The same goes for writing. By at once dwelling in the mystery and containing it, writing makes life occasionally beautiful, nearly tolerable.

A nice conspiracy is afoot here, as readers, too, revel in mystery. Writers get better at the craft once we learn to assume that the reader will do much of the work for us, filling in the blanks with their own experiences and lives. Plant a few key pieces of evidence, and your reader will dream up the connections. It's what Darwin did, after all—he was one hell of a mystery writer. It's what we do with all of our own invisibles. As the prosecution held at the first O. J. Simpson trial, the absence of evidence does not constitute evidence of absence.

Still, living in the mystery is not the same as floundering in it. There is an underlying purpose to a writer's detective work, I believe, which has to do with catching bad guys. I know this may sound like an extravagant claim, corny too, but I think that we writers enjoy tromping around in the murky zones of good and evil, right and wrong, justice and injustice, so that in the long run, we may settle on the good, the right, and the just. We may traffic in murder and madness, and cultivate the seediness of the private op. But when it comes down to it we want to rescue our reader-clients, however surprised we may be to rediscover our innocent sense of honor every time we string words together.

At heart, most of us are Sam Spade in *The Maltese Falcon,*

when he is about to hand over the many-aliased Brigid O'Shaughnessy to the cops for killing his partner, Miles Archer. She asks if Archer meant more to him than she does. She loves him, she says, and he loves her. He says he doesn't know if that's so. But he lives by a code. "When a man's partner is killed," he says, "he's supposed to do something about it. It doesn't make any difference what you thought of him. He was your partner and you're supposed to do something about it." When a man's partner is killed, "it's bad business to let the killer get away with it. It's bad all around—bad for that one organization, bad for every detective everywhere." His struggle is moral. He won't let her go free "because all of me wants to." His decision is practical. "And because—God damn you—you've counted on that." The plain truth is that Miss O'Shaughnessy is evil, which makes her his enemy. She asks if he would have acted so high-minded if the black bird had proved real and he had been paid his money. He says: "Don't be too sure I'm as crooked as I'm supposed to be. That sort of reputation might be good business . . . making it easier to deal with the enemy."

All writers are mystery writers. We may not employ detectives in our work, but as seekers of guilty parties, we can identify with Nick Charles, Sam Spade, Lew Archer, Miss Marple, and the rest. Like them, we muck about in a world studded with clues, neck-deep in motives. Like them, we falter in our investigations and follow wrong leads. We are foolhardy, preposterous, nosy, irritating. No one wants us around. We work alone, yet like Sam Spade, we operate within a tradition of our own, of which we are respectfully aware. Write and you are in the company of all who have written before you. Only when we have finished a piece of work do we know true shame is loneliness, realizing that the chase is over and that no one has been watching us but us.

A movie for writerly romantics appeared in the 1970s, called *They Might Be Giants,* with George C. Scott as a glorious nutcase who thinks he's a modern-day Sherlock Holmes, and Joanne Woodward as his psychiatrist companion, Dr. Mildred Watson.

Throughout, Scott pursues Professor Moriarty, Conan Doyle's personification of evil, along New York's streets until at last, in the final scene, he confronts his nemesis, who confronts him back. I was no longer a boy when I saw that movie, but I was still in the detective business, though my office had shifted location to a desk and a soft chair, and I wore a legal pad, not a cap gun, near my chest. Here I remain for as long as I am allowed, as the cloud-ghosts shroud the skull of the sky, and the air trembles, and the figure of a man, huge and obscure, turns to face ridiculous me.

{ essay in *The New York Times Book Review* }

If You Are Strange Enough, They Will Come

A good idea is to cultivate at least one wholly unreasonable facet of your behavior and to force more reasonable people to accommodate themselves to you. I, for example, do not use a word processor—in part, for some sound reasons and, in part, for no reason at all. I do my writing on a yellow legal notepad and then on an electric typewriter, for which I have cornered the market on typewriter ribbons. Of course, there is no market for these items other than myself and, perhaps, a dozen other oddballs. And I know that I really should start using a word processor and stop making life a chore for those who are cursed with handling my work.

Why do I persist? Not to be quaint. Not to be difficult, though I realize that I am. I cultivate this wholly unreasonable facet of behavior because I want things my way and because I know that, sooner or later, if I do not budge, people will bend their lives to mine. If I am strange enough, they will come. Editors never question why they must put my materials into the system for me. They have simply found it expedient to adapt to my strangeness, mainly because I have never indicated that I would adapt to them.

One ought not to carry such behavior too far or others will grow restive and resistant, and you'll be cooked. And I do not advocate developing an eccentricity simply to amuse oneself or for the sake of tormenting others. But if you like doing something your way—no matter how odd that way might be—the world will heel.

The candy emperor, Forrest Mars, was the creator of M&Ms, and he insisted that the *M* on every M&M be printed in the exact center of each piece of candy. Often he would phone a sales associate in the middle of the night if he found that an *M* was not where it should have been, and he would order the candy to be recalled. Employees bristled. Mars died in 1999. Go out and get an M&M. Note where the *M* is.

{ from the instruction book *Rules for Aging* }

From the Memoir
The Boy Detective

In Pennsylvania, on an overnight at summer camp, a bunch of us boys strayed from the group and went for an evening walk, on which we came upon a deserted farmhouse. One lame-brained kid, who used to amuse himself by pulling the legs off frogs, casually tossed a rock at an upstairs window. He missed. Another boy came closer, his rock hitting just below the sill with a slap. Then all the boys picked up rocks and hurled them at the empty gray farmhouse. Its paint was peeling. It stood like a headstone against the slate of the sky. A few minutes passed. I watched the others throw their rocks, and considered whether or not I wanted to join in. Then, for no reason I could think of, I picked up an especially good rock and threw it at that upstairs window. I was a pitcher. I did not miss.

Drink in the fresh-mowed grass. Grind the dirt under your cleats. Stare in. Turn away. Do we ever leave our childhood? "Roger is a good athlete" read my second-grade report card. "But he doesn't like to play with the other children." More problem than compliment in that, since most of the sports one plays require the cooperation of other children. Consider the person who can play with his peers but chooses not to, and so is left in a self-confounding position—he who stands alone among other players, elevated, the center of attention who is at the same time ignored by his teammates, expendable and indispensable, at once in and out of the game.

The thing about pitching, about being a pitcher, is that you want to make the batter appreciate what you have thrown at him, but only briefly, a glance. You don't want to taunt him. You let the ball do that. And then he looks away, as in a dream, having coming to terms with the fact that the only way to understand what you have done is when it is too late for him to do anything about it. Like detective work. Like writing.

From the Unpublished Memoir
Unaccompanied Minor

Underneath his temperament, the pitcher is the team writer. You see it in the windup, when he's about to toss the ball, and he pauses, stopped in air. At this moment, everything is possible. He addresses the batter as the writer addresses the blank sheet of paper. The ball will travel inside or outside, high or low, or down the center of the plate. It will be hit squarely, fouled off, or missed entirely. Any result may occur. So the pitcher pauses on his perch and dreams of what he will write. And if a disaster ensues, and the ball goes sailing over the centerfield fence—if his writing falls flat in its face—he still has that one moment in the process, posed in his wind-up, when everything will turn out just as he has hoped.

From the Novel
Thomas Murphy

Sometimes I forget what a delightfully curious fellow I am. And then I do something that reminds me. This morning, for instance, I took down every one of my poetry books—others' books, not my own—from the floor-to-ceiling bookcase reserved for poetry, in the front hall. I took them down one at a time and I opened each to a random page. There must be seven or eight hundred books on my shelves—from old Tu Fu to Yiddish poems to the work of Phillis Wheatley, Edgar Guest, Julie Sheehan, William Empson, Daniel Halpern, Marianne Moore, and others. I have 'em all. I laid all the open books on the floor of the hallway, with a foot or two between the rows, so that I could patrol the lot of them and read a line or two on each open page. Sometimes I happened to open a book to a complete poem, sometimes to isolated stanzas. I read the lines aloud, as if the entire haphazard arrangement on the floor constituted one very long organized poem.

So, I read some lines of Shakespeare, then moved on to Mark Doty, thence to Poe, thence to Countee Cullen, and Billy Collins, and Emily Dickinson and Frost and Southey, and Galway Kinnell, and on and on. There were no connections among the passages, and nothing made continuous sense. But the accumulation of the total work had an effect, nonetheless—like a collection of all the comments one might hear from a crowd viewing a monument, Lenin's Tomb, for instance, or coming upon an amazing natural sight, say, Niagara Falls, rising in and filling my front hall from floor to ceiling.

I shouted, "the wound is open" from Anne Sexton. I shouted "the mad in absolute power" from X.J. Kennedy. I shouted "it was not a heart, beating" from Sylvia Plath, and "I remember these things I still remember them" from Apollinaire, and "some things are truly lost" from Richard Wilbur, and "went you to conquer?" from Donne. I shouted "what is articulated strengthens itself" from Milosz. I loved that so much, I shouted it twice. The exercise occupied most of the morning, if you include the time I used in taking down the books and putting them back. Afterward, I sat in the kitchen, with my toast and coffee, pleased with myself, I don't know why. I can't recall thinking about the poets' lines I'd read. I was not studying them, and they certainly were not studying me. Principally, I was more aware of the sound the accumulated lines made, senseless, illogical, beautiful. What is articulated strengthens itself. We simply had been keeping company with one another, comforting one another, me and my fellow poets, in the morning, in the front hall.

From the Unpublished Memoir
Unaccompanied Minor

Where and how I discover Louis Untermeyer's anthology of modern poetry, I cannot recall. I am fourteen, maybe fifteen. But once I come upon the small, thick, bluish book that contains the work of all the important poets of the era, I carry it around like a Baedeker's. The names alone are poems to me—Moore, Cummings, Tate, Millay, Eliot, Ransom, Crane, Aiken, Witter Bynner. Who but a poet could be called Witter Bynner?

Jones Very. Is that a whole name or part of a name? Mr. Untermeyer put himself in his anthology, which I think tacky but clever. How else would anyone ever know of the poetry of Louis Untermeyer? I come across Isaac Rosenberg. Close.

Auden is my favorite. I memorize "September 1, 1939." Also, "Lullaby." I learn that Auden lives near where my parents grew up. I stand at St. Marks Place and look across the street at the six-story sandstone building I am told is Auden's. I do this once or twice a week, after school. Just stand there and stare, in the heat or the cold.

Writers are my rock stars. Tennessee Williams is staying at a windmill that is part of an inn in Southampton, where my parents go on vacation. I am fascinated by him as he moves alone between the mill and the main house, appearing only in the early evenings for a drink at the great oak bar, always in a summer jacket and tie. Self-sufficient, self-composed, he sits at the far end of the bar, nursing a gin. His gigolo mustache nearly makes him look lascivious, but his character lies in his thoughtful, steady gaze. From time to time another guest approaches to pay him a compliment. He is always gracious, but indicates by his body language that he is not seeking company. I lurk in the arching doorway of the bar, watching Mr. Williams and wondering what it is like to be a famous writer. Once he smiles at me, but there are no words between us. I go to the flagstone terrace as the sun sets, look out at Shinnecock Bay, and wait. After a while, Mr. Williams leaves the main house of the inn and walks back to the mill and his splendid isolation.

From the Book-length Essay
The Book of Love

I have not loved the world nor the world me—Byron at his touchiest. I give to you and you give to me—nothing. Yet something is insincere about this famous yawp. If the poet hadn't loved the world, why did he give a damn if the world loved him back? He would have omitted the second part of the line. Why would anyone in his right mind care if the world showed its love? That sort of display only turns your head, and gets you nowhere. Loving without expectations of reciprocity, on the other hand, well, that gets you everywhere. What's more: In the following stanza, Byron backs off, conceding a little here, a little more there, until he winds up hoping "goodness is no name, and happiness no dream."

But never mind all that. Isn't the world just too damn big to love? Unwieldy. Who could get his arms around the bloated bastard, with all its floods and quakes? Who could go for that? Better to love the world for its towpaths, weeds, and blackbirds. Your slightest look easily will unclose me—Cummings at his loveliest. Love the world not for its bigness, but rather for its slightest looks, its smallest gestures. A wave, for instance. Strangers waving to one another, hands raised briefly, making a fraction of an arc. On a towpath, say, past some weeds, beneath an umbrella of blackbirds. From your sullen arms I extract a wave.

One heart we have with poets. One memory of the world. One wish for the world. They forgive us everything.

From the Novel
Thomas Murphy

O ver the rock fields I climbed to Synge's Chair—that formation of rocks shaped like a caveman's throne, where J.M. Synge is said to have brooded his plays and essays into being. Synge's Chair. Have I told you about this? That great granite head of his, and the iron mustache. I would trudge to Synge's Chair, yearn toward the Atlantic, remain till nightfall, and mark the red declension of the sun. Then I'd return home and my da would read to me in my bed. My unshaven, baritone da of the red creased neck and whiskey breath. He would prop his one existing leg on the low stool in front of the fire, and read me Padraic Colum and James Stephens, and sometimes even Kavanagh, when da was in his cups.

His favorite was Yeats. He'd read me the early poems, easier for a boy to understand, such as "At Galway Races," "These Are the Clouds," and "Brown Penny." He loved "Brown Penny"—a young man's poem, he said—and he recited it from memory. Lusty, wistful, plain sad sometimes, as he'd glance as his left leg, then at the space where his right leg used to be. He'd lost that one in a thresher, when he was eighteen. He never complained, never a word, just that glance at the absent leg. More than the books, that taught me how to write a poem.

They really aren't difficult, my poems, no matter what the good Dr. Spector says. Greenberg got 'em readily enough. Oh, I'll toss in a wild word from time to time, to keep the reader on his toes, the way Heaney does, and Paul Muldoon. But neither of those great fellas is hard to understand, and I'm not either. Most of the poets of my race are not hard to understand. We just play hard to get.

Basically, we're piano bar players, singing our guts out and writing by ear. Which is probably why the ancient Irish poets were known in their kingdom as The Music. Poets were called The Music. When the kings did battle with one another, which was every other day, they dispatched their soldiers with orders to kill everyone in the enemy camp, every man, woman, and child, including the opposing king. Kill 'em all, said the king. Except The Music. The soldiers were forbidden to ever kill The Music. Because he was The Music.

Metaphor and Simile

I love you the pewter way the creek looks in a light rain. I love you the brown way of that anomalous tree, the wavy one between the taller pines, in our backyard. I love you the luscious way a plum tastes on an afternoon when one sees a plum on a plate and unconsciously grabs it. I love you the frail, sure way of daisies, the shiny kettle way of French press coffee, the breezy way of September, the resigned, determined way of "September Song." And the touching way of a dog's face, I love you that way, too. And the moth beating its wings on the window way. And the anticipatory way of a conversation, when the one you're with is about to tell you something new about the etymology of a familiar word, or an idiom like "the devil and the deep blue sea," or about themselves. I love you that way as well. I love you the way one changes one's mind about having dessert, the way a bus has a hissy fit before a stop, the way you tie a bandage on your finger, or on mine, the way a book falls open to a reference to Chaucer. I love you the way horses snort, ducks bat their wings, the way e. e. cummings loves, the way Doris Day sings, "It's Magic," the way baby boomers go gooey at a James Taylor concert outdoors, on a lawn. I love you that way and this, hair up or down, sneakered or well-heeled, shouting or sleeping, tired or more tired, the way you look tonight or any night. How do I love thee?

{ from the book-length essay *The Book of Love* }

From the Memoir
Kayak Morning

Words mixed with water lose their bite. They do not help. Old words, or new, now, they do not help. I had believed otherwise. If you could say it, or write it, if you could give shape and expression to it, clarity and precision to it, then something good would come. Now I skim. I flip my words. They spin me into silence, all my light and darkness wordless. My therapist friend would tell me that it's all for the good, like righting a kayak by deliberately rocking yourself off balance and nearly toppling into the creek. Like the postwar jet pilots who, trying to break the sound barrier, crashed when they pulled the stick back but sailed through when they pushed the stick forward. Skipping similes like stones.

The mind is like a kayak.
  That's a simile, all right. But what do you mean?
  The mind is like a kayak. It prods and pokes about.
  Very good. Anything else? It points. Also travels in circles.
  Excellent. The mind is like a kayak.
  You're making fun of me?
  Not at all. You're king of the similes. Only I was wondering . . .
  Yes?
  Does it alter the creek?

From the Unpublished Novel
Young Murph

Patrick Kavanagh looked at me seriously, for once. See here, Thomas Murphy, he said. You want to be a poet, and who am I to try and stop you. But I can tell by the dumbass light in your eyes—the way you talk about *me*, for Chrissakes—that you think poets can actually do something in the world. That poetry has this beautifyin', civilizin' power nothing else has. Shelley called us the unacknowledged legislators of the world. I'm here to tell you, we are no such thing, acknowledged or unacknowledged. It's a crock.

Poetry changes not a goddamn thing, Thomas. It does not make the world any kinder, freer, or more sensible. It doesn't affect the unspeakable or the merely stupid. It doesn't even make people more alert to poetry. All the poems ever written and to be written—the poems of John Keats, the poems of Thomas Murphy—could vanish tomorrow, and no one would be the wiser. Ya (he begins to amuse himself), I can picture some dumb bunny in Kerry or Mayo wakin' up, panic and alarm in his big blue eyes, and shouting to whomever else is in the house, Where are the poems? Anybody see the poems? William fucking Blake thought his work was of national importance. National importance!

Can't you just see it?! Black-faced miners risin' from the darkest shit holes of the earth, and clambering for the latest Blake. Gimme that tiger! Gimme that lamb! In a pig's eye, boyo. You can have your Blake and your Walt Whitman, your Ezra Pound, and your goddamn Paddy Kavanagh, too, bless his rotten soul—poets as different from one another as grains of wheat—nothing that ever happened in the world, good or bad, can be traced back to a single one of us.

And I'll tell you something else, my hepped-up friend. It ain't just poems that are useless, it's language itself. Words. There are no words for the deepest things we feel.

Think about that. No words. Scrawny old Sam Beckett was on to something. So you and I and all the highfalutin poets of the world strut about with our pathetic divining rods, poking the bulrushes for the right word, the absofuckinglutely right word—the little beauty, the gem—when in fact the right word is never to be found. Because it doesn't exist. The very stuff we want most to express can never be expressed. No words, Mr. Murphy. Put that in your thesaurus and smoke it.

But if there are no words, Mr. Kavanagh, I said meekly, why do the civilizations of the world exist? Hah! He laughed and fell into a coughing fit. Civilizations, Thomas? There are no civilizations. Never have been. That's just a word we invented to make us feel good about ourselves. History, my boy, is made up not of civilizations but rather teenage gangs marauding and swaggering from continent to continent, destroying everything that gets in their way. Women and children first. Then, when they stop in one place and settle down for an hour or two, taking a breather from their slaughter, one of them writes a poem, and they call what they have, civilization. And no sooner does everyone read the poem and nod and grin in self-satisfaction, that they pick up their daggers and clubs again, giddy with power and ready to do each other in. Civilization?

The life closest to civilization is when people keep their mouths shut, like the Neanderthals, and their poets keep their mouths shut, too. Tape 'em tight. Sew up the lips. That's why I'm tellin' you, young Thomas Murphy, I'll never write another poem as long as I live.

Do you not believe, I said, that poetry can rescue people, bring them out of their sorrow when they're desperate and want to do themselves in? Or when they just need to know that everyone suffers?

Rescue? He said. Rescue? Show me an instance where anyone has been rescued by a poem, lad. So you're lying around dyin' and who struts up but Big Willie Wordsworth, toting the Lucy poems. "A Slumber Did My Spirit Steal." "Oh, Mr. Wordsworth!" says Tommy Murphy in his parched and quavering voice. "I'm dying!" and Wordsworth says, "That's why I'm here, young Thomas. To read you 'A Slumber Did My Spirit Steal,' and bring you back to life." "Well," says Tommy, "that's grand, Mr. W. But please don't read 'The Prelude,' too. I'll be in the ground two weeks before you finish the first half."

Much as I disagreed with Mr. Kavanagh, much as I wanted to quote my da and prove Mr. Kavanagh dead wrong, I must tell ya, he did his playlet beautifully—his tongue sticking out of his mouth when he was speaking for the dyin' me, his nose in the air for Wordsworth. Tell me, boyo, he said. Did Dr. Jesus read a poem when he was raisin' Lazarus? You got to get your feet back on terra firma, Tommy! No poem in the history of poems ever rescued a cat up a tree.

Nature Writing

I have often been in this spot, and of recent years I have felt that this might be the last time that I should look down from here upon the kingdom of the world and their glories; but see, it happened once again, and I hope that even this is not the last time that we shall both spend a pleasant day here. In future we must often come up here.

That was Goethe to his friend Eckermann on September 26, 1827, as the two men sat on the grass and had a picnic at Buchenwald.

{ from the essay collection *Anything Can Happen* }

From the Memoir
Making Toast

The dead have occupied much of my time this past year—books and poems about the dead, conversations with other families about their dead. I read death into innocent remarks and innocent texts. At the time it feels accidental, but I know it is not. I should try to get away from the subject. It is not infinitely interesting, as thinking about it ends only in a grim shrug. In any case, there is more to do. And I grow weary of my anger.

My wife, Ginny, and my son-in-law, Harris, may feel that their lives have prepared them for our current circumstance. I do not. I doubt that my life has prepared me for any situation, because until my daughter, Amy, died, I had always believed that good things would simply befall me. Except for a few disappointments, probably less than my share, I've led a charmed life. I am learning what most people know at a much younger age—that life is to be endured, and its rewards earned. Since my rewards these days lie in the survival of my family, I am content to try to earn them.

But all this comes slowly to me. I have not been a long-distance runner, and now—at the time when my legs are weak and my wind diminished—I need to confront the long haul, which runs counter to my nature. I must train myself to deal with the world as it is, as Amy did, while not treating the assignment as a chore. One of the few pieces of writing I have done since Amy died was a book review for *The Washington Post Book World*. The novel was David Lodge's *Deaf Sentence*—about a retired linguistics professor, Desmond Bates, who is losing his hearing and who is also deaf to life until, against his will, he visits Auschwitz, where the silence teaches him to hear. He reads a letter from a prisoner in the camp to his wife, discovered in a pile of human ashes. One sentence rises up to Desmond:

"If there have been, at various times, trifling misunderstandings in our life, now I see how one was unable to value the passing time." As far as I can tell, this is how to live—to value the passing time.

Snow on a Beach

On a weekend for which a light dusting was forecast, a good four inches fell on Quogue. They wouldn't call four inches snow in places like Butte and Fargo, but on the southern shore of eastern Long Island the amount is impressive. It makes a sudden New England of an area that, in fact, was settled before most of New England, in the mid-seventeenth century. The steep roofs of the New England–like houses are lathered with snow, and the surprisingly tall pines are shagged with ice, the way they get in Vermont. The main difference is the beach. There is snow on the beach.

I walk there on a Sunday morning. The snow draws a wide lateral strip at the top, and where it stops, the sand, brown and wet, continues to the lip of the ocean. I suppose the tide washing ashore made that portion of the sand too warm and moist to sustain the covering of snow, so half the beach is snow and the other half sand.

Sights like these are jarring to the senses, yet they make sense to writers, because our experience as well as our craft tells us that certain things, in and out of nature, do not belong together. One of the great tricks of writing is to toss disparate, unconnected things in the air, and let the reader attempt to do the connecting. Snow on a beach startles the imagination. Writers seek to startle the imagination.

Students of my generation were taught to value E. M. Forster's dictum "only connect." It was assumed that making connections was a sign of the mind's worth and purpose. Only connect; things fall apart; these fragments I have shored against my ruins. Perhaps this effort to bridge and yoke was a consequence of growing up under the persistent threat of disintegration from nuclear craziness. Perhaps it was simply an invention of the academy in which exam questions insisted on one's making sense of this as related to that. We are naturally antianarchic, prounion.

Some years ago, I was watching the Academy Awards on one channel, staring at the shimmering people. And then I flipped to another channel where the news was showing some eighty dead bodies swaddled in body bags on the floor of an auditorium. They were the victims of the Happy Land social club fire in the Bronx. Flip: the Academy Awards.

Flip: the dead of the Bronx. I wondered how these things fit together in the world. Would there be a movie made of the Happy Land fire? Would it win an Oscar?

So I sympathize with people who seek to create a unity of thought and emotion out of disorder, but I also believe that trying to fit parts into a whole makes each component smaller, less interesting, and inauthentic. There is a life of parts as valid as the life of the whole. Simply noting is often enough. What right have I to give the universe a shape other than the one in which it presents itself without comment? The world steps forward as Dennis Rodman more often than as Grant Hill, bad as it wants to be, still loco after all these years.

The sad truth (is it sad?) is that no great story ever makes sense, nothing important is to be understood, and no part fits. Homer was blind, Beethoven deaf. Blake's wife couldn't read. And I am that stumblebum on the beach, loving you.

{ essay in *Time* magazine }

From the Memoir
Making Toast

Mrs. Salcetti invites me to visit my granddaughter Jessie's second-grade class, and talk about writing. I know Luxmi, Arthur, and Jaraad from last year's first grade. I tell the kids I have memorized all their names, and make up a new name for each of them, calling boys Phyllis, girls Ralph, and so forth. My nonsense coupled with their cries of protest eats up ten minutes. I look over at Mrs. Salcetti. "Am I through?" I ask. She smiles, and points to the clock. "Only forty minutes to go," she says.

At her insistence, I tell them the plot of my first novel, *Lapham Rising,* sanitizing it a bit, but staying true to the essentials. Naturally, they are way ahead of me. They analyze the characters I merely describe, noting possible nuances. They explain the theme of my book to me. I become adept at nodding. I have them begin a novel of their own. "Write a first sentence," I tell them. "And remember, you want the reader to be very interested right away." Jessie writes, "Once upon a time, there was the best-behaved class in the world." I ask the children, "From that one sentence, what do you think is going to happen in Jessie's novel?" Practically all of them shout, "They're going to be bad!"

From the Novel
Lapham Rising

To the good people of Chautauqua:

I'm sorry I will not be able to be with you for your program on the twentieth century. But I'm dead. I would like to take this postmortem opportunity, nonetheless, to tell you about the lecture I cannot deliver in person.

Are you ready to hear this, Chautauquans? Are you sitting down? Yes, of course you are. You're always sitting down.

A loud pop from a burning log startles me, and I turn to see the fire gobbling up my cord of wood, then rushing to the hill like panicked horses, and spreading everywhere. This is not the best atmosphere for writing. But it does add a certain urgency, a real deadline. I continue:

My lecture was to be about Lapham, my sordidly ambitious, absurdly self-important, earsplittingly noise-making, unwanted neighbor, Lapham. For anything you want to know about the destructive, witless twentieth century, you may look to Lapham. Every time you see a monument to personal glory, some dumbass splurge at the expense of taste and good works—some house, for example, that is thirty times larger than it needs to be—there's your twentieth century for you, and your twenty-first to boot.

So just say it: Lapham. Scream it: Lapham. Wear a button: Down with Lapham.

Paste a bumper sticker to your fender: no laphams on board.

Now the air is clogged with smoke. I try to fan myself with my legal pad, but it doesn't work. I'm going to get this done regardless.

The foregoing, in a nutshell, my Chautauquans, was to be my lecture—a plaint-cum-fire-and-brimstone oration, a call to arms against my neighbor and his ilk, who with their incessant banging and their flabby dreams have taken away my world, the world I wanted to hang on to.

And what was this world I wanted to hang on to? Why, dear Chautauquans, it was *you,* your world of thought and of art and of friendship and of usefulness to others. Perhaps that last above all: usefulness to others. For no other reason would I have come to you to speak. And when your invitation arrived the very day that Lapham began to build his house, I knew then that I would have something to tell you, especially you who, in your slightly pixilated but fundamentally lovely way, hold fast to the same world that my parents and their parents before them tried to preserve within the little band of the Marches, down through time.

But here comes the sad part of my lecture. For I had hoped to inform you that against all odds, I had defeated Lapham, reversed his upward direction, or at the very least slowed him down. Indeed, my original intention was to relate to you a tale of conquest, and to suggest how each of you might make that tale your own. Yet to my sorrow and embarrassment, I must report not on my victory but rather his. The fact that I am dead speaks for itself. And the object lesson I have learned, after all the high-flown theorizing and the gathering of evidence, and all the clever conclusions that the mind is capable of, is that the Age of Lapham—in all its vapidity and self-regard, in all its empire building and vanity, in its mindless dollars and its most powerful air conditioner in the world—wins.

Just that: it wins.

As if to support my conclusion, the heat from the fire has grown ovenlike. Where is the Tillis Blowhard outdoor air conditioner when you need it? More popping of logs.

When I turn around this time, all I see behind me is a sky in flames. Perhaps this is more atmosphere than I needed. Only a few sentences to go.

So what lesson may I bring you, my worthy Chautauquans, as I picture this letter of mine being read to you, seventy-five hundred strong, sitting in your vast amphitheater— and read to you, what's more, by two teenage interns who came across my message in a vodka bottle as they were making out on your beach? The lesson is this: the reason Lapham has won this time, and will win again, and will always win, is that *you* allow it to happen. You sit together in your amphitheater, but you do not stand together.

Rise up, Chautauquans. (I stand for dramatic emphasis.) Rise up to defend your world of thought and poetry and music and your lacy red-and-blue porches stuffed with gladiolas and your leafy glades and your true-blue lakes. Rise as Lapham is rising, and smite him not with weapons—they will backfire, take it from me—but rather with your books and your songs and your laughter. Beat him back with your modesty, the knowledge of your frailty— that is to say, with your humanity.

Or if you prefer, you all can go out and live on your separate islands and seethe and fume and rant and go nuts in the company of your sarcastic, barking Bible-thumping dog. It worked for *me*.

From the Unpublished Memoir
Unaccompanied Minor

Even as a child, I tend to seek the writer's aloneness. I am six. Rutherford Platt, a renowned naturalist, is taking his sons, Ruddy and Andy, along with me and a group of the neighborhood boys for a nature tour of Central Park. The group swings one way and then the other, like sheep herded by a dog. I am lagging in the back. Then Mr. Platt and the other boys are gone. Just like that. And I am standing on a path alone, as bicyclists wheel by. I make no effort to catch up with the group. Instead, I wander, taking note of everything around me, especially the people. Families with baby carriages. Solitary walkers. Lovers tilting toward each other. A park custodian with a garbage pail on rollers greets me cheerily, and moves on. Finally (after an hour? Ten minutes?) a tall policeman spots me, escorts me to the park station house, and gives me an orangeade. He speaks into a microphone on a desk. "We have an unaccompanied minor." He calls out my name and describes my clothing.

Soon Mr. Platt and the others show up at the station house. I am glad to see them, though as I walked, I never was fearful. We lost you, says Mr. Platt, looking something between terrified and studious. Or did you lose us?

Better Angels

Oh, what the hell. Let's go for it. Let us speak about great writing—not brilliant writing or clever writing or, most tempting of all, exquisite writing. Let us speak of Quixote writing, Lear, and Deronda writing. Honor, heroism, decency, justice, and "Ah, love, let us be true to one another" writing. Gaah! The very words are marzipan to the tongue.

And yet, at the end of the day—our own or days in general—what else do we seek from our books? The verities need not be expressed gently, unambiguously, or in rhyming couplets, but it is the verities that make us know ourselves. And you can swoon your critical head off over Joyce's bourgeois *Ulysses* and Robert Graves's girl-crazy "Ulysses," and still know in your acritical heart that neither holds a candle to the original wild sailor or even to Tennyson's old salt, who strove, sought and found, and did not yield.

When I start thinking this way, I wonder if I'm just growing old, and tired of modernity. Yet even when modernity was young, I was captivated more often by clarity than by calculated difficulty, and pleased simply by someone doing a far, far better thing. It is always thus for most of us, I think. Whatever brief delights it provides, mere strangeness in poetry and prose eventually leaves us cold, especially when we suspect the writer is stretching for effect to avoid the actual life before his eyes. (As if people were not strange enough.)

Why, for example, do the great writers use anticipation

instead of surprise? Because surprise is merely an instrument of the unusual, whereas anticipation of a consequence enlarges our understanding of what is happening. Look at a point of land over which the sun is certain to rise, Coleridge said. If the moon rises there, so what? The senses are startled, that's all. But if we know the point where the sun will rise as it has always risen and as it will rise tomorrow and the next day too, well, well! At the beginning of *Hamlet* there can be no doubt that by the play's end, the prince will buy it. Between start and finish, then, we may concentrate on what he says and who he is, matters made more intense by our knowing he is doomed. In every piece of work, at one juncture or another, a writer has the choice of doing something weird or something true. The lesser writer will haul up the moon.

There have been times in literary history when writers steered clear of the great moral issues, but not completely, and never for long. The eighteenth century (Johnson, Gray, Cowper) had no problem telling people how to think and behave. The Romantics made the egotistical sublime, though Wordsworth's self was large enough for everyone. The Victorians opened things up again, as did T. S. Eliot a little later, with big pronouncements about the state of the world. Literature took to the confessional in the 1960s, when personal demons took over for universal evils. Yet while Robert Lowell and Sylvia Plath shrank colossal subject matter to the size of Czar Lepke and Daddy, we still could see the Us in Them. One might say that the shadow of the Big Bad Bomb made honor, heroism and the rest beside the point. But *Invisible Man* and *Doctor Zhivago* appeared while we were ducking and covering, suggesting that dealing with big themes in literature depends less on eras than on individual inclination.

So, let us speak of Fitzgerald, and of Jay Gatsby, who stood straight and sober in the drunken Twenties, and who, nutty as his yearnings may have been, really was great. And this was not because he was willing to take the wheel and the rap for the moral nitwit, Daisy. That was more gallantry than heroism. No. Gatsby showed his splendid colors in a quieter gesture, when he decided to stand watch outside Daisy's house after the hit and run, thinking to protect her from Tom—dear Daisy, who at that same moment was sitting across from Tom, over a plate of cold fried chicken, the two of them in the "natural intimacy" of their dreary conspiracy. Behold Gatsby, the hero of the useless heroic vigil.

Small wonder Nick does not understand when Gatsby dismisses whatever passed for love between Tom and Daisy as "just personal." The great Gatsby lives above the merely personal. Could there be any doubt that he was "worth the whole damn bunch put together"?

Let us also speak of Dickens, who is often undervalued because he hits the eternal verities on the nose. Sure, we cannot help being aware of his in-your-face morality, yet we are moved by it nonetheless, because, tossing sophistication to the wind, we wish to see the just rewarded and the unjust punished. No writer besides Shakespeare has created more memorable characters attached to vices and virtues. And the two authors have similar aims. In even their least sympathetic characters, one senses a kind of helplessness to passion quivering between the poles of good and evil. Both Miss Havisham and Mrs. Macbeth probably would have preferred to behave themselves.

As whimsical and uproarious as they could be, Dickens and Shakespeare took life seriously and sought moral truths—and with all their other gifts, that is why they were great. Among our contemporaries, see E. L. Doctorow, Cynthia Ozick, Richard Wilbur, Philip Roth, Doris Lessing, Seamus Heaney, Alice McDermott, Richard Ford, and on and on, though not indefinitely. Whenever we pick up the work of any of these people, we know without looking that the subject will be important, that something "of certain magnitude" (Aristotle) is at stake. In "Preface," Czeslaw Milosz said that "serious combat, where life is at stake, / Is fought in prose," adding, "It was not always so." It is not always so in prose, either. But we welcome the strife, which may pit woman against herself (Jane Austen) or man against Troy. Style? I cannot tell you if Twain or Tolstoy was a great stylist. The lesser excellences of great writers do not occur to us, because what those writers have to say is overwhelming. They shoot to the sun, and leave us blinded, ecstatic.

A curious line in Auden's elegy to Yeats applies to writing great: "Teach the free man how to praise." Auden seems to be saying that freedom, used most typically for carping and revolt, might also acknowledge that the world is worth thinking well of. The writers we admire most are propelled by a mixture of innocence and chutzpah—the nerve to write big coupled with a childlike need to cultivate the virtues they have always believed in. They may surprise themselves by the insistence of their own higher motives and values. They may also believe that as readers, we will surprise ourselves for the same reasons.

Why else would eyeless Milton have decided to move heaven and earth to appeal to our better angels? Let us speak of Milton, and our better angels.

{ essay in *The New York Times Book Review* }

"I Am Writing Blindly"

Besides the newsworthy revelation of Lieutenant Captain Dimitri Kolesnikov's dying message to his wife, recovered last week from the husk of the sunken submarine Kursk—that 23 of the 118 crewmen had survived in an isolated chamber for a while, in contradiction to claims by Russian officials that all had perished within minutes of the accident—there was the matter of writing the message in the first place.

In the first place, in the last place, that is what we people do—write messages to one another. We are a narrative species. We exist by storytelling, by relating our situations. And the test of our evolution may lie in getting the story right.

What Kolesnikov did in deciding to describe his position and entrapment, others have also done, in states of repose or terror. When a JAL airliner went down in 1985, passengers used the long minutes of its terrible spiraling descent to write letters to loved ones. When the last occupants of the Warsaw Ghetto had finally seen their families and companions die of disease or starvation, or be carried off in trucks to extermination camps, and there could be no doubt of their own fate, still they took scraps of paper on which they wrote poems, thoughts, fragments of stories, rolled them into tight scrolls and slipped them into the crevices of the ghetto walls.

Why did they bother? With no countervailing news

from the outside world, they assumed the Nazis had inherited the earth; that if anyone discovered their writing, it would be their killers, who would snicker and toss them away. They wrote because like Kolesnikov, they had to. The impulse was in them, like a biological fact.

So enduring is this storytelling need that it shapes nearly every human endeavour.

Businesses depend on the stories of past failures and successes and on the myth of the mission of the company. In medicine, doctors increasingly rely on a patient's narrative of the progress of an ailment, which is inevitably more nuanced and useful than the data of machines. In law, the same thing. Every court case is a competition of tales told by the prosecutor and defense attorney. The jury picks the story it likes best. The only reason O.J. got off in his murder trial was that the jury preferred Johnny Cochran's story to Marcia Clark's. Adding the ridiculous to the horrific, O.J. finally went to jail for stealing his own stuff.

All these narrative activities derive from essential places in us. Psychologist Jerome Bruner says children acquire language in order to tell the stories that are already in them.

We do our learning through storytelling processes. The man who arrives at our door is thought to be a salesman because his predecessor was a salesman. When the pattern-making faculties fail, the brain breaks down. Schizophrenics suffer from a loss of story.

The deep proof of our need to spill, and keep on spilling, lies in reflex, often in desperate circumstances. A number of years ago, Jean-Dominique Bauby, the editor of *Elle* magazine in Paris, was felled by a stroke so destructive that the only part of his body that could move was his left eyelid. Flicking that eyelid, he managed to signal letters of the alphabet, and proceeded to write his autobiography, *The Diving Bell and the Butterfly,* with the last grand gesture of his life.

All this is of acute and consoling interest to writers, whose odd existences are ordinarily strung between asking why we do it and doing it incessantly. The explanation I've been able to come up with has to do with a mysterious sort of freedom. You write a sentence, the basic unit of storytelling, and you are never sure where it will lead. The readers will not know where it leads either. Your adventure becomes theirs, eternally recapitulated in tandem— one wild ride together. Even when you come to the end of the sentence, the dot, it is still strangely inconclusive. I sometimes think one writes to find God in every sentence. But God (the ironist) always lives in the next sentence.

It is this freedom of the message sender and receiver that connects them—sailor to wife, the dying to the living. Writing has been so important in America, I think, because communication is the soul and the engine of democracy. To write is to live according to one's terms. If you ask me to be serious, I will be frivolous. Magnanimous? Petty. Cynical? I will be a brazen believer in all things. Whatever you demand I will not give to you—unless it is with the misty hope that what I give you is not what you ask for but what you want and need.

We use this freedom to break the silence, even of death, even when—in the depths of our darkest loneliness—we have no clear idea why we reach out to one another with these frail, perishable chains of words. In the black chamber of the submarine, Kolesnikov noted, "I am writing blindly." Like everyone else.

{ essay *in Time* magazine }

Words on Pieces of Paper

Picture Shallus doing the words, "engrossing" the Constitution, as the process was called, copying it out at an elegant angle in large, legible script. The four sheets of parchment were vellum, the skin of a lamb or a calf, stretched, scraped, and dried. The ink, a blend of oak galls and dyes. The light, an oil lamp. The instrument, a feather quill. All nature contributing to the assignment, human nature in the form of Jacob Shallus, ordinary American citizen, son of a German immigrant to Philadelphia, soldier, patriot, father of eight, and, at the time of the Constitutional Convention, assistant clerk to the Pennsylvania General Assembly. The convention handed Shallus the documents for copying on September 15, 1787. He had forty hours to transfer the four sheets of parchment, 4,440 words, for which the payment was thirty dollars, good money for moonlighting.

Two centuries later Shallus becomes history's triviality, his story faintly revived by a scholar, Arthur Plotnik, in a new biography. But the words on paper are given Bicentennial parades. Amazing little artifact. What started out at one man's writing desk eventually journeyed the country from city to city as the nation's capital moved, went into hiding during the War of 1812, was transferred from federal department to department until it wound up in the National Archives in Washington, sanctified in helium and watched over by an electronic camera conceived by

NASA. The quill age to the space age, and at every stage, a nation full of grateful believers making a constant noisy fuss over a piece of writing barely equivalent to a short story—much theme, no plot, and characters inferred.

Call the Constitution literature? Sarah Orne Jewett once wrote to Willa Cather, "The thing that teases the mind over and over for years, and at last gets itself put down rightly on paper . . . it belongs to literature." One would have to say that the Constitution qualifies, human minds having been teased for centuries with the possibility of making a government that would allow that mind to realize itself. The document shows other literary attributes as well: a grounding in the ideas of its time, economy of language, orderliness, symmetrical design, a strong, arresting lead sentence. Then, there's all that shapely ambiguity. Even those who have never have read the document—enduring wars, debts, threats to health, privacy, equality, down to questions raised by AIDS and aid to the *contras*—are convinced that the Constitution's words foresaw all that.

Which, in a way, they did. The Constitution is more than literature, but as literature, it is primarily a work of the imagination. It imagined a country: fantastic. More fantastic still, it imagined a country full of people imagining themselves. Within the exacting articles and stipulations there was not only room to fly but also the tacit encouragement to fly, including the instructions to fly, traced delicately within the solid triangular concoction of the framers. Even two hundred years after the fact, when people debate whether the Constitution is fit for so complicated and demanding a time, Americans take as granted the right to grow into themselves. They must have read it somewhere, in a fable.

Still, picture Shallus, before any of the hopes were raised

or satisfied, the four skins laid out before him, the ink, the quill, and the lamp. And the words, like mysterious ciphers, handed over to him by the best minds of the age, who had just sweated out a Philadelphia summer to claim intellectual territory, which was to translate to a civilization. Did Shallus read what he had copied when he finished? Would he have understood it if he had? How could he dream that all those words, thought out so meticulously, were conceived only for him? Citizen Shallus bent over his desk in his country, deliberately, exquisitely in the act of being born.

{ essay in *Time* magazine }

From A Letter to the Year 2086

In some ways, then, we are giving you the future in this letter, which seems a right thing to do for one's children's children's children. Look back to us as we look to you; we are related by our imaginations. If we are able to touch, it is because we have imagined each other's existence, our dreams running back and forth along a cable from age to age. Hold this paper to the light. It is a mirror, a delusion, a fact in the brief continuous mystery we share. Do you see starlight? So do we. Smell the fire? We do too. Draw close. Let us tell each other a story.

{ essay in *Time* magazine }

From the Novel
Thomas Murphy

Are you out there? The cry of poets everywhere. Are you out there? Meaning, not merely you at this minute, but you who exist a hundred, a thousand years from now. Are you reading old Murph, Sir Thomas James Murphy, Esq. himself. DEA, PCP, SUV, KFC?

Have I done anything worthy of reaching across the plains of the years to you in your dumps or palaces? I see you walking in the stubbled fields, heads down over a book. A book! Still? Is it *The Collected Works of Thomas J. Murphy* you're reading, or, if not all the works, a work or two, a phrase or clause, perhaps a single word quoted in your version of *Bartlett's*. Even a plagiarized idea will do. Or have the secret police banned any mention of my name. Something?

Show me the palms of your hands. Show me on Skype. Nothing. The leathery puckered palms of your two-fingered hands. Nothing. Have you no interest in what went before? I may not be much, but I went before. My head teems with galaxies. Someday, in the year 5014, you too will have gone before, and if you write a poem, you too will ask, Are you out there? Of course, it is possible that at this stage of erosion you know nothing, including your own desires. You may have evolved to eyeless petunias marooned at the farthest edge of the Isle of Lusitania, where there is only fog and skulls, in a place so desolate, it makes Inishmaan look like Metropolis. Yet, if you do not read me, if you do not read anyone, why kiss?

Rumors of your existence have reached headquarters. Before the mass suicides that ordinarily attend such bulletins, you might send word that someone is reading someone somewhere. Even if you have to make it up. Here I gladly abandon my ego. If nothing of mine survives, so be it. But Wallace Stevens? What of Wallace Stevens? Surely he must have tunneled his way out of the camp, enduring the critics and other fecal matter, and found his way to you, bearing a poem or two, a line or two, or a thought. He said that poetry reveals appearances and renovates experience. Something worth preserving in that. No? Health. He said poetry is health. To your health, then. *Sláinte*. Cover your nostrils and your eyes. What is that *howling*? You?

Hard to believe that all our excursions end in ice. If I have a past, I have a future.

My projections are contained in my time capsule. Within me I hold what is to come. I need not see it. Poetry should carry my future, even if the anthologies are airy, and the range of colors is reduced to gray, and there is no light in you. No light. Then read by my light, the light of me, by my flickering hope that by some means of transport, in the pebbles and the terns, shivers urgent news of me and mine. You are my tongue. You are my poem. Are you out there?

From the Memoir
The Boy Detective

Writing is unreasonably demanding. A tyrant, a regular Stalin, when you get down to it. Why do I have to produce an ocean in the morning, much less paint the sun-streaks on it, much less the plaster clouds or the goddamn sun itself? What do you take me for, anyway—a court magician, a wizard in a stupid star-splashed dunce's hat? A down-and-out sketch artist on lower fifth on a Sunday afternoon, awaiting your ten bucks so that I might make your chin more manly or give you a nose job in charcoal? I'm not God, for Chrissake, or Christ, for God's sake. I'm not your father, either, if that's what you're thinking, and even if I were your father, aren't you old enough by now to fetch your own ocean? Oh, never mind. I'm just venting. You didn't create this case. I did. I, and the smirking sheet of paper that says, in the greasy voice of a racetrack tout, how about an ocean this morning, pal? Yeah. And make it original.

From the Memoir
Making Toast

After the July Fourth weekend, my wife, Ginny, my son-in-law, Harris, and the children return to Maryland. My granddaughter Jessie and grandson Sammy are eager to get back to their Wii, a virtual reality video game that Harris got them at the start of the summer. I need to stay on in Quogue for the Southampton Writers Conference, which extends from mid-July to the end of the month. The writers, who also teach workshops, pair up for the evening readings. This summer I am partnered with Frank McCourt. Frank reads from his first work of fiction. I had thought to read from my novel *Beet,* which had come out in February. But while looking for something in a tangle of papers, I came across an essay I'd written for *Time* twenty-one years earlier, called "Speech for a High School Graduate." It was an attempt at a literary commencement speech, written to honor my daughter, Amy. I wrote similar *Time* essays for my sons, Carl and John, upon their high school graduations, using the trope of a father giving his personal commencement speech to his children as he looked to their future.

I decide to read the essay instead of the passage from my novel. I would not have done so for an audience of strangers, but Bob Reeves, the conference director, and my good friend, has fostered a familial atmosphere over the years, and the participants have grown close. When Amy died, Billy Collins wrote us, "Sometimes there *are* no words."

Frank, Lou Ann Walker, Meg Wolitzer, and others stayed in constant touch. Melissa Bank sent a little package containing a floral handkerchief for Ginny, audiotapes of short stories for my drives, and a chestnut she had found in the driveway of a restaurant in Tuscany some years ago, which had given her comfort. I do not think the essay to Amy will feel inappropriate. So after Frank finishes, I read what I had written when Amy was seventeen. It interests me how many of my wishes for her had come true—her love of travel, of animals, of music, her appreciation of history, her enthusiasm for sports, her respect for traditions. I wished her fierceness in battle but urged her not to hang onto corrosive enmities. I wished her a love of work, predicting that it would have "something to do with helping others." I wished her productive solitudes, and worthy friends, though in her case that wish was superfluous. I wished her the pleasure of an exchange of wit with a stranger, and moments of helpless hilarity. I wished her life in a place where she might see a stretch of sky. The essay ends with a promise never to let go.

A Writer's Speech for a
High School Graduate

Your official commencement speaker tackles the big themes, tells you to abjure greed, to play fair, to serve your community, to know thyself. Your more personally devoted commencement speaker agrees with all that.

But he has special wishes for you, too, a writer's wishes, which have to do with ways of seeing the world, of living in it, and not quite on it. Some of these wishes are weird, of course—what an educated daughter may have come to expect from an oddball. People have always said you resemble him.

What he wishes you first is a love of travel. Travel will hold you back from doting on your troubles, and once you've seen something of the world, you will recognize foreign places as instances of human range. The logic of Athens, the fortitude of London, the grace of Paris—a city for every facet of the mind. He would have you connect travel with an appreciation of the past as well. In Jerusalem recently, he walked the Old City, brushing thousands of years of faith and murder. He would like you to see yourself as history, to wonder what you would have shouted, or at whom, as Jesus struggled up the Via Dolorosa. He hopes that you will husband your own past, too. The past means possibility.

He also wishes you a love of animals, which you feel strongly already; he hopes that tenderness lasts and grows.

Animals, too, draw people out of excessive self-interest, their existence a statement of need. A dog's eyes search your face for a mystery as deep as God, asking nothing and everything, the way that music operates. He hopes that you always love music, even the noisy boredom you clamp to your ears these days, while he harbors the prayer that in later years will follow Vivaldi and Bix Beiderbecke. If you learn to love jazz, you will have a perpetual source of joy at the ready. Jazz is serious joy, much like yourself.

For some reason, he has always favored culs-de-sac, so he hopes you live on one, someday, a neat little cutoff that surprises the city's motions with a pause. Trees on the street, he would like that for you, and low modest houses so the sky is evident. He hopes that your mornings are absolutely still except for birds, but that the evenings bulge with human outcry, families calling to one another in the darkening hours. He wishes you small particulars: a letter received indicating sudden affection, an exchange of wit with a total stranger, a moment of helpless hilarity, a flash of clarity, the anticipation of reading a detective thriller on a late afternoon during an electric storm.

He hopes that you learn to love work for its own sake. You have to be lucky for that (of course, he wishes you luck), and find a job that grows out of dreams. Something to do with helping others in your case, he should think, since he has seen your natural sympathy at work ever since your smallest childhood and has watched you reach toward your friends with straightforward kindness. Friends, he knows, you will have in abundance. He wishes them you.

He hopes that you will always play sports, just as ruthlessly as you play sports now. He hopes that you will always seek the company of books, including the trashy romances; that you will always be curious about the news, as long as you do not mistake the news for life. Believe it or not, he even hopes that you will always be crazy about clothes, particularly once you establish your own source of income—fashion plate, charge plate.

You seem to know the difference between vanity and style. On you high style looks good, kid.

Eccentrics: he hopes that you always have plenty of them about you, and few, if any, sound thinkers. Sound thinkers appear on television; sycophants award them prizes for sound thinking. Eccentrics have a sound of their own, like the wild Englishman Lord Berners, who invited a horse to tea, or less extravagantly, Bill Russell, who played basketball to meet only his own standards of excellence. Russell told his daughter that he never heard the boos of the crowd because he never heard the cheers—no easy feat in an age pumped up by windbags. Your commencement speaker hopes that you will turn a deaf ear to empty praise as much as to careless blame, that you will scare yourself with your own severity.

Solitude he wishes you as well, but not solitude without a frame. Choose creative times and places to be by yourself. In museums, for instance, where you may confront Vermeer or Velazquez eye to eye. On summer Sundays, too, when you may be alone with the city in its most clear and wistful light: the mirrored buildings angled like kitchen knives, the Hopper stores dead quiet, the city's poor dazed like laundry hung out to dry on their fire escapes. For contrast, seek real country roads, tire-track roads straddling islands of weeds and rolling out into white haze. Such roads are not easy to find these days, but they exist, waiting to trace your solitude back into your memories, your dreams.

You never back down from a fight. Your commencement speaker cheers you for that, and hopes you do not weaken or think safe. Still, it helps to learn that some fights are too small for kindling, and if you must fight out of your weight class, always fight up.

Hatred without a fight is self-consuming, and fighting without hatred is purposeless, so regretfully he wishes you some hatred too. But not much, and not to hold too long. There is always more cheapness in the world than you suspect, but less than you believe at the time it touches you. Just don't let the trash build up. And there is much to praise.

Such as your country, which he hopes that you will always cherish, that you will acknowledge the immeasurable good in the place as well as the stupidities and wrongs. If public indignation over the scandals in Washington proves anything, it is that Americans remain innocent enough to believe in government by laws, and to be angered by deceit in power. He hopes that you retain and nurture that innocence, which is your country's saving grace.

In general, he wishes that you see the world generously, that you take note of and rail against all the Lebanons of violence, the Africas of want, but that you also rear back and bless the whole. This is not as hard to do as it may seem. Concentrate on details, and embrace what you fear. The trick is to love the world as it is, the way a father loves a daughter, helpless and attached as he watches her stretch, bloom, rise past his tutelage to her independent, miraculous ascendancy. But you must never let go entirely, as he will never let you go. You gave birth to each other, and you commence together. Goodbye, my girl.

{ essay in *Time* magazine }

151

Do Not Go to Your Left

Going to one's left—or working on going to one's left—is a basketball term for strengthening one's weakness. A right-handed player will improve his game considerably if he learns to dribble and shoot with his left hand and to move to his left on the court. What is true for basketball, however, is not true for living. In life, if you attempt to compensate for a weakness, you will usually grow weaker. If, on the other hand (the right one), you keep playing to your strength, people will not notice you have weaknesses. Of course, you probably do not believe this. You will want to take singing lessons anyway.

We punish ourselves with the cultural expectation that the highest achievement in life is to be a "renaissance man" (or woman). The oddity of this designation is that there were precious few people in any renaissance (Italian, English, or Irish) who could do more than one thing well. (Pace, Michelangelo.) What they did well, they did surpassingly well. I don't recall Dante creating anything that held a candle to "The Divine Comedy." Shakespeare, Marlowe, and Kyd could write plays *and* poems, but in those days they were much the same thing. Yeats couldn't write great plays any more than Synge could write great poems. None of the renaissance men gave a moment's thought to his left.

Writers, establish your strength and strengthen it. English critic Hilaire Belloc advised that a young and aspiring writer "concentrate on one subject. Let him, when he is 20, write about the earthworm. Let him continue for 40 years to write of nothing but the earthworm. When he is 60, pilgrims will make a hollow path with their feet to the door of the world's greatest authority on the earthworm. They will knock at his door and humbly beg to be allowed to see the Master of the Earthworm."

To be sure, Belloc was specifically addressing the writer "who is merely thinking of fame." But what writer is not? Find thy earthworm.

{ from the instruction book *Rules for Aging* }

From the Memoir
Kayak Morning

My therapist friend refers to *Making Toast* as a sort of guide and corrective to my current state of mind. This feels strange to me. When you've written and published a book, it goes out like a child sent into the world. When you reread it, it seems as if it were written by someone else, which is true, since, like a creek, we move on naturally. The other day I was in a lecture hall, about to give a reading of *Making Toast,* and the man who introduced me told the audience that he was impressed with the book's sure commitment to life. I could not look up at him when he was speaking of me, because I know I am weaker than my book.

Is That All There Is?

Years ago, I was on a panel with Russell Banks, and we were talking about *Affliction*. Russell was pleased with the novel's reception, but he also said he'd hoped he was creating a worthwhile body of work. This was not said with a dismissive attitude toward the appreciative things people were saying about *Affliction*. Rather, it seemed that Russell was stepping back, surveying all he'd done to that point, and keeping a careful eye on the whole even as readers were concentrating on one recent part.

Readers and writers do not think of a body of work in the same way. To a reader, a body of work is a static totality by which a writer may be assessed. To a writer, it is something of a taunt. Writers think of a body of work as a movie tough guy whom we have popped in the jaw. We rear back and deliver our best haymaker, and the body of work shakes it off and says, That all you got?

For this and other reasons, writers generally do not like to read their work once it is published. We find mistakes. We find things that make us cringe. And the whole process kills whatever momentum we may be feeling. The body of work becomes a body of evidence in a case built against us. We find a writer we barely recognize, and who seems to want to pick a fight. See all our books lined up on the shelf. They are a museum, a graveyard. They are a chorus line, arranged side by side like the Rockettes. All that's missing is the kicks.

Good or bad, a particular piece of work does not say anything lasting to us. We finish the poem, novel or memoir, send it into the public air, and think about what to do next. The collected work, on the other hand, says a great deal to and about us. It usually says we have been weighed in our own balance and found wanting. Collectively, our body of work is an expression of implied yearning. And while we may be full of ourselves while producing the poem, novel, or memoir—drunk on the power of language or subject matter, and buried in laughter or fury or whatever we're dreaming up at the time—when we come up for a breather, there sit the words settled on the page, unmoved and unmoving. Is that all we got? Hear us sigh.

Last summer, I lost two great friends, and the world lost two great writers, James Salter and E. L. Doctorow, both of whom created lasting bodies of work. Jim went first, having collapsed during a workout. We had dinner the night after his ninetieth birthday, and got soused on zombies. Edgar died a few weeks later, after fighting lung cancer for a year before pneumonia did him in. Not long before he died, he went for a checkup at Yale, where he was receiving an experimental treatment. Did you wow them in New Haven? I emailed him on his return. Not only did I wow them, wrote Edgar. I huzzahed them, I yippee-ai-ayed them and I mazeltoved them!

Shortly before his Yale trip, on a still, summer afternoon, I visited Edgar at his home in Sag Harbor. He talked about a piece he'd seen that called *Ragtime* the great American novel. Half playfully we inventoried his other novels to see if they deserved the title over *Ragtime*. (My candidate was *The Book of Daniel*.) Edgar wasn't taking all this too seriously.

But it was interesting to rove through his body of work with him, because he did not wish to dwell on it. In fact, ill as he was, he had an idea for a new short story, the prospect of which put life in his eyes. The point is, he would not see his body of work as an adamant structure. Though monumental, it was to him a work in progress till the end, the perpetually evolving yearning of a monumental soul.

This statement of yearning may be why the term "body of work" is applied equally to one who has produced a tremendous amount of material, and to one who has written only a few things. The difference between a minor and a major poet has to do with quality, not heft. Allen Ginsberg is a major poet for no reason other than "Kaddish." Djuna Barnes, Ralph Ellison, and Joseph Heller created a very few books, yet each produced a body of work. Elizabeth Hardwick could rest her case with *Sleepless Nights*. When a writer has said all that he or she has to say, or as much as possible before mortality intercedes, the body of work remains incomplete no matter the size of the output. Peggy Lee at the mic—"Is That All There Is?"

I don't think longevity affects the relationship with output, either. I doubt that Wordsworth at the end of his long life was more satisfied with his body of work than was Keats, at the end of his short one. In a way, all writing is essay writing, an endless attempt at finding beauty in horror, nobility in want—an effort to punish, reward and love all things human that naturally resist punishments, rewards and love. It is an arduous and thankless exercise, not unlike faith in God. Sometimes, when you are in the act of writing, you feel part of a preordained plan, someone else's design. That someone else might as well be God. And then one day you rear back and survey everything you have done, and think, Is this all God had in mind? But it's all you got.

{ essay in *The New York Times Book Review* }

From the Memoir
The Boy Detective

Except for the chains, I would not mind being a prisoner in Plato's cave. The allegory has it that the prisoners were bound and limited by more than chains because they could not see reality, and thus were deprived of the truth. They could see only the shadows of the puppets that the puppeteers cast on the cave's wall, and believed that the shadows were the puppets themselves. Being unable to turn their heads, they knew nothing of what caused the shadows. If they had seen the shadow of a book, say, or of a man, they would have mistaken appearance for reality—a destructive and unforgivable error, according to Plato, and the theme of most of modern literature, according to university professors.

But is this so? See here: I recognize that man walking across Park Avenue South toward the Starbucks on the northwest corner of Twenty-ninth Street under the lurid light of a streetlamp. It is Sidney Homer, the man whose apartment on the ninth floor of 36 Gramercy Park mirrored our own. A Wall Street investor, he is the son of Marian Homer, the opera singer, and the grandson of Winslow Homer, the painter. When I was four or five, he used to greet me in his booming voice and ask when I planned to enroll at Harvard. When I got to Harvard eventually, the Homers gave me a leather-bound early edition of Johnson's dictionary, which I keep today in an antique book press. So there is Mr. Homer, tall and elegant, striding across the avenue to get his morning coffee. I see him clear as day-light, though he died thirty-five years ago.

Would you say that he is less real to me than the young man in the baseball cap advertising the *Today* show, who actually is crossing to Starbucks? The shadow of Sidney Homer is cast upon the wall of my mind's cave. "What is REAL?" The Velveteen Rabbit asks the Skin Horse, who answers that when you are loved, you begin to become real. "Does it happen all at once, like being wound up?" asks the Rabbit. "It doesn't happen all at once," said the Skin Horse. "You become. It takes a long time. That's why it doesn't happen often to people who break easily, or have sharp edges, or who have to be carefully kept." If one wants to get technical about it, the Rabbit is no more real for having been loved, or for growing old. Yet only strict Plato would say that he does not represent the truth. They say that no one ever survives old age, but that is hardly true. To the Aborigines, dreaming was the way to prolong the life about them. Here on this walk, I dwell in an eternal gloaming, just like you. We survive and love in an ageless present.

From the Memoir
The Boy Detective

Something Faulkner said in *Light in August:* "Memory believes before knowing remembers. Believes longer than recollects, longer than knowing even wonders." So does this mean that a memoir is an act of faith, and that the various worlds we write into creation represent our way of making a heaven and a church—all the things that receive belief? A god itself? We might ask ourselves why this form of writing exists. And the answer may be that the memoir is an instrument by which we redo our lives in order to have something to believe in. As unhappy or confused as our memories may be—as chilling or terrifying or just plain sad—the accretion of them, nonetheless, becomes a kind of altar at which we worship. The structure constitutes our salvation. Quasimodo cried out to the cathedral of Notre Dame, If only I were made out of stone like thee. The church, our Lady of Memory, becomes our sanctuary.

Which is to say, students, your memoir is not about you. So, stay out of it. Keep clear of your memoir, except in those instances where your idiosyncratic, weird, freakish life speaks for others, for all lives. As you write, let your mind wander to subjects outside your worries, shames, griefs, traumas—no matter how devastating or exciting they may be—to history, plain facts, abstract thoughts, and to the people for whom you write. At the outset of a memoir, you are propelled by the desire to let the world know who you are. Soon you will discover that you don't really care that much about who you are, and that writing with that goal alone will turn boring, cloying. You will tire of yourself just as you tire of others who think only of themselves, and whose chatterings are mere perseverations of autobiography.

I'll say it again. Your life is not about you. Or to put it more usefully, it is about the you in you that is common to everyone. Your life is about everyone. In his tender *An Autobiography,* the poet Edwin Muir describes his emotional awakening after undergoing psychoanalysis for the first time. "I saw that my lot was the human lot," he writes. And "in my own unvarnished likeness, I was one among all men and women." To see that is not only to acknowledge something essential about one's life. It also serves the writing of the memoir by diverting the reader's attention from the one to the many, while at the same time, the one uses the many to try to discover who the one really is and what his story is about. Your memoir is not about you. You are the world in which you walk, you and everyone else.

It's Not About You

I n the late 1970s I was writing columns and editorials for *The Washington Post*. Because I knew nothing about any particular subject, it fell to me to write the paper's editorial whenever a prominent person died. So frequently did I write such pieces, that I soon became known by my colleagues as "Mr. Death"—not the most cheerful nickname, but at least it indicated a minor skill.

When Golda Meir passed away, Mr. Death was called upon to write an homage to her life and accomplishments. Rather than recite known facts, I wanted to get at least one quotation from someone who had known her personally. I was referred to a very powerful columnist of the time, whom I phoned with my request. "Could you tell me something especially revealing about Mrs. Meir?" I asked him. "Oh, yes!" he said at once. "We were very close, you know. I shall never forget the day she leaned forward and told me: 'You are, without question, the best columnist in America.'"

It was fascinating to realize that this man—accomplished, admired, intelligent, worldly-wise—had not the slightest idea of how ridiculous he sounded. (I did not use the quote.) But what came off as merely a silly thing to say probably concealed a worldview; this fellow actually believed that all questions were about *him*. Trust Mr. Death: It's not about you—particularly when the "it" has to do with someone's demise.

A few years ago, I went to a memorial service for a revered book editor and a very good guy. One by one, authors with whom this editor had worked came up to the pulpit in the church to speak of the deceased's mind and character. One eulogy went: "'John,' he once said to me, his eyes moist with tears, 'you are the best writer since Hemingway!'" Another: "'Mary,' he said, trembling from head to foot with joy, 'you are the best writer since Virginia Woolf!'" And so on.

I recall another memorial service where a man talked for nearly a half hour, recounting various tales of how much the dearly departed had relied on his excellent judgment.

It's not about you is a simple rule to follow if you concentrate on the question or the occasion at hand and ask yourself: What is required here? Though you are certain that you are the center of the universe, you might acknowledge, in one or two instances, that you ought to travel to another planet. Modern journalism has not been much help is supporting this rule, which may be why is seems archaic. These days it is the way of journalism to assume that the story is only about the journalist—a media version of provincialism. It is normal today to read a newspaper story about a political assassination that begins: "I was feeling queasy that morning when news of the king's death reached me. Maybe it was the coffee."

Frank O'Connor, the great Irish short-story writer, used to speak of his relationship with Yeats, in part to elevate himself by association. It was all good-natured, if transparent.

Before Yeats died, O'Connor would recall that "Yeats said to me . . ." After the poet's death, O'Connor turned the recollections around: "I said to Yeats." I studied briefly with O'Connor in Dublin. And I shall never forget the day he told me: "Roger, you are the best writer since me and Yeats!" Such a wise man, O'Connor.

{ from the instruction book *Rules for Aging* }

Time Is, Time Was

If you don't like this review, blame John Banville. I was all set to keep my nose out of the thing, disliking, as I'm sure you do, those literary appraisals in which writers—out of a cheap competitiveness or an unseemly eruption of self-esteem—decide to make the review about themselves. But with *Time Pieces,* how could I resist? I lived in Dublin in the mid-1960s, when Banville was also there. We were close to the same age and walked the same brooding streets and strolled around the same St. Stephen's Green and browsed in the same melancholy brown-and-purple shops, crossed the same bridges with the lace-iron gates, drank in the same pubs, including McDaids and the Shelbourne Hotel's Horseshoe Bar, and took in the same Georgian houses and the same black-silver canals and loitered in the same libraries and heard the same rich talk and met some of the same people, but not each other. We both were taken by Harold Nicolson's diaries and shared the minor lament that neither of us could afford to eat in Jammet's, the most expensive restaurant in town.

Even recognizing these coincidences, I vowed to keep my proper distance until about halfway through the book, where Banville writes of Nelson's Pillar, the granite column erected as a monument to Lord Nelson's victory at Trafalgar that, to the irritation of many Irishmen, had towered over Dublin like a gloating Colossus from 1809 until March 8, 1966. That was the day a crew from the IRA blew it up in an act of sabotage so surgically efficient no one was hurt, hardly any damage was done to the surrounding buildings, and the admiral's head was lopped off clean as a chicken's.

On that March morning, Banville was "jolted out of sleep" by the "distant thud" of the explosion, and I, living at a greater remove in the suburb of Mount Merrion, heard about the event on the radio. Off I went to O'Connell Street to see what I could see. A good bit of the pillar remained intact at the base, stone chunks here and there, and the head, with its chipped nose, lips, and forehead and a socket of an eye, looking like Yul Brynner's in *Westworld,* had rolled off to the side. I found the whole daring business thrilling and published a poem about it in the *Irish Times.* It was less thrilling to an older Irish woman whom I overheard, standing beside her companion and surveying the open space where the monument had been. "Och, sure," she said, "it was always gettin' in my way, anyway."

Reading this delicious memoir, how could I keep from wondering: Was Banville on the same spot that amazing morning? Was he standing near me? Was he the one I nodded to in the tacit exchange of two astonished and impressed young men? All those long long years past, and now I'm back with Banville, happily, admiringly, with only the debris of time scattered around us.

So, *Time Pieces.* The title is a four-way pun, I believe, referring to wrist and pocket watches, pieces of writing on the subject of time, fragments or units of time, and the assemblage of memories that time pieces together, such as this memoir. Banville's book is about time, insofar as a memoir is about anything, and about the past particularly, of which Banville is an honored citizen. In his Benjamin

Black crime novels, he often takes up residence there, as he did in early novels like *Kepler, The Newton Letter,* and *Doctor Copernicus.* In the recent novel *Mrs. Osmond,* his sequel to *The Portrait of a Lady,* he extends the past as he picks up Isabel Archer's story where Henry James thought he'd ended it. It's no surprise, then, that in *Time Pieces,* Banville asks himself, "When does the past become the past?"

Driving around town with his friend and travel companion Cicero, in Cicero's little red roadster, he becomes the flâneur with wheels, greeting the past as he goes. He touches on the pain of leaving Dublin as a boy after a visit to his aunt, hiding his tears on the train ride home to Wexford because "something was ending" and thus becoming the past. He also veers into old Dublin as he writes of the preserved stones of the Abbey Theater, destroyed in a fire in 1951, and pauses for a recollection of Georgie Yeats, the poet's wife, and her penetrating black eyes that glanced at Banville "straight out of the past." In a house on Henrietta Street, he notices a fragment of wallpaper whose survival unaccountably reminds him of the ruins of Herculaneum, sections of which were preserved in volcanic dust, spared from the lava flow that destroyed Pompeii. "How many imbricated layers of the past am I standing on?" he wonders, an echo of an earlier quote he recalls from Rilke: "But this / having been once, though only once, / having been once on earth—can it ever be cancelled?"

It never can be. The only tense we live in is the past. The present moves so fast that it becomes the past even as it's observed and experienced. And the future is, well, the future. And since the people, events, and objects of our little histories are never commonly agreed upon—I saw it one way, you saw it another—the past becomes endlessly interesting, as changeable and unnerving as any work of art. Perhaps childhood never leaves us because we were pure artists then, unfettered by much personal history.

Childhood fascinates Banville because it's "a state of constantly recurring astonishment." When the astonishment ebbs, the past clouds over into itself. "The process of growing up," he writes, "is, sadly, a process of turning the mysterious into the mundane." Only when the adult artist revives it are we excited at the prospect of what is long behind us.

Yet memory is oddly selective. "I recall so many trivial things," Banville proclaims, "and forget so many very momentous ones." In memory, the seemingly insignificant becomes so insistently prominent, who can tell if we have any idea of what is really important? One of the points of Bruegel's "Landscape with the Fall of Icarus," perhaps the main one (pace Auden), is that the ordinary townspeople who ignore the divine hotshot's spectacular plunge are also suffering. To Banville, an apostle of the ordinary, the deep appeal of city life is that here the ordinary may be made magical.

His book is about the past, and about people worth bringing back. Not just the members of his family but figures like the kind and sympathetic assistant librarian Miss Flushing, "with her magnificent conical breasts poking against a pale-blue angora jumper." And, most movingly, the actor Micheál Mac Liammóir, who, along with his partner, Hilton Edwards, a theater impresario, founded the Gate Theater, where Orson Welles got his start. The two men went about as "the most prominent, not to say the most flagrant, representatives of the homosexual life of Dublin." The city, Banville says, was unusually accepting of gays, and Mac Liammóir and Edwards were beloved public figures. In an age like ours, when the streets are paved with eggshells, Banville does something that's both touching and embracing—especially with Mac Liammóir, who never went out in public without wearing "makeup and a black wig that glistened like wet coal." He shows the actor's brilliance and wit within his gayness, not apart from it.

Pity the fool who's reading this book to get a clear and orderly picture of Dublin. But oh, what a topographical map has been drawn by Paul Joyce's evocative photographs and Banville's observant eye. Like Max Morden in his Man Booker Prize–winning novel, *The Sea,* Banville remains willfully and gloriously disorganized. The tour he takes us on, while offering a handful of interesting facts about Dublin, is more about moods and states of mind and how they shape, even create, the so-called real world. "I have never in my life paid much attention to my surroundings," Banville writes, alert, in the way of Joyce, not to what people do but rather to "what they are." As he puts it, "Art is a constant effort to strike past the mere daily doings of humankind in order to arrive at . . . the essence of what it is, simply, to be."

So, like the more thoughtful Romantics, Banville sees into the life of things. Autumn, he concludes, is more expectant than spring because the "stealthy tumult of the dying season" causes it to tremble with love. A fringe of gray curls on the head of a nearly bald man looks like "a fallen-down halo." Standing by the canal at Lower Mount Street Bridge, he watches a heron, "awe-struck by the clean sharp dangerous lines of the thing." (He makes *thing,* that most unmoored of words, sound precise.) On a May morning, "the pale sky shines and shimmers like the inner skin of a vast soap bubble." He recalls Stephanie, an alluring young woman whom he spotted when he too was young. She was "slight, with an almost boyish figure," and her long dark hair was parted in the middle. It was love at first sight—his, alas, not hers. Years later, when he meets her again, his swain's heart gives an "anguished quack." And once again he feels "the unutterable enormity of love pressing hotly behind one's breastbone like a hot lump of lead."

Banville's soarings, like a hawk's, are both wild and comprehensive, taking in everything and imagining more. One can't distinguish his descriptions from the things described, the dancer from the dance. See how he gives us the Great Palm House of the Botanic Gardens with its walkways "high above our heads, among the upflung fronds, narrow, perforated metal platforms that must surely lead to diving boards." One "would not be surprised should there come a sudden splash followed by a swimmer streaking down in an arc and skimming past us, making fish-mouths with his hands—his palms!—pressed together above his head." In that same Palm House, the philosopher Wittgenstein is commemorated by a plaque for the time he lived in Dublin in the 1940s. Banville cites him on several occasions in *Time Pieces*. Wittgenstein believed that language isn't separate from reality.

The better memoirs tend not to be principally about the suffering of the author but rather about what the author has noticed in his or her life, what is cherished or abhorred—often about pure information worth imparting. The better memoirs are the more generous, looking outside the self. I don't think it's an accident that the photographs of Banville in this book are shot from behind, showing him looking away. *Time Pieces* is subtitled *A Dublin Memoir* to signal that the author is focusing on the city.

Here Banville feels at home, just as I did all those preposterous years ago. Banville says he was once told at a dinner
party that there's no such thing as a coincidence. So I am
given a book to review, written by the splendid novelist
with whom I shared a wondered staring at Lord Nelson's
detached head, both of us standing on the imbricated layers of the past and each about to blunder hopefully into
our separate unimaginable lives.

{ review in *The New York Times Book Review* }

From the Play
Ashley Montana Goes Ashore
in the Caicos

T he inventor of time.
If no one had invented time, everything would
happen all at once. Your birth, your schooling, your
outrageous behavior at prom, your marriage, the birth of
your children, the scorn of your children, your éclaircisse-
ments, your denouements—all would occur in the blink of
an eye, and everything in life would be accordioned like
the paper sheath of a drinking straw, just before a drop of
water turns it into a writhing snake.

But this simile is so inadequate. It is impossible to imagine a world without time, where no time hangs heavy,
and no hands have time on them, and no one serves time
because time serves no one, and there are neither the best
of times nor the worst.

Someone, you see, had to think it up—a Cro-Mag-
non, perhaps, after he had knocked off the Neanderthals
because they could not speak and were a waste of something. Perhaps it was one who noticed that this moment
was not like the previous moment and who conjectured
that the next moment, the moment to come, was likely to
be different as well.

I like to think of that person: The mother-to-be who
watched her belly swell from month to month and realized that something miraculous was going to emerge; the
artist who, displeased with the red ox he had just painted
on the wall of his cave, realized that he could do another

picture later; or the hunter who, as the lion was about to leap on his head, realized that something was not on his side.

I could spend hours wondering who that person was, and how he or she realized in a flash of invention, that from then on, there would be a then on, and a there was, and an is.

Oh, hell. I'll say what I mean. I want more time.

Poems and a Prisoner

I don't think anything that has been
created can be destroyed.
  —Sy Jackson on immortality

It hardly looks troublesome these days, this odd, 1930s fortress with the Greek-echo name, but in September 1971, Attica put hell on display for the nation. There are no signs of prisoners rioting today. The shock to one's system lies simply in the place itself, its main wall rising thirty feet around fifty-three acres in the middle of dead-quiet upstate greenery. The wall is gray gray. Nothing in nature, including a rock, could be that color. Guards say the foundation of the wall goes down thirty feet in spots so as to hold fast in the quicksand. At intervals along the flat surface, watch turrets sit with witch-hat tops; Disney World, had it been built by Albert Speer, would have this look. The wall encompasses five separate cell blocks. Inside these are individual cells, seven feet from floor to ceiling, nine feet by six feet in area, in which some two thousand men live among the possessions permitted them.

Sy Jackson sits hunched over at the tail end of his narrow cot. At five feet eleven inches and slightly more than two hundred pounds, he ought easily to fill his cell, but he seems to have willed a diminished appearance in order to stay in proportion with his furnishings. Most of these hang on the walls: a chain of beads, a pair of sunglasses, snapshots of his three children. He has copied William Ernest Henley's poem "Invictus" by hand and mounted it with cellophane tape. There is a picture postcard of a sailboat at sunset below what Sy calls his "mind stimulators," words of advice on how best to study: survey, question, read, review, recite. Between the postcard and the sunglasses lies a poetic formula:

You imagine *what you desire*
You will *what you imagine*
You create *what you will.*

For the most part Sy believes you create what you will, but he also believes one creates what others will for him. The stony face he wears now—the wary eyes resting on the bulging cheekbones, the rare smile that never shows wide enough for warmth—it was not always his look. In Elmira, he says, "I learned how to be hard and cold. I was neither before. I used to dislike fighting so much that if I ever did get into a fight with a kid, I couldn't even hit him in the face. That's the God-honest truth. Then in prison I went through a transition, as if I was beginning to understand another side of human nature, in myself as well as others." Specifically, he learned that generosity was interpreted as weakness. A fellow inmate at Elmira borrowed five packs of cigarettes and refused to pay Sy back. Sy fought him. "It wasn't my nature, it was survival. I would have thrown that guy out the third-floor window."

There is no doubt of it. Even today you see the indignation rising in him as he recalls the cigarette borrower. He talks with his hands; a swallow would be lost in them. Transferred to Comstock after the Elmira incident, Sy was involved in another fight for which he says he was given forty-five days in the "strip cell" (one meal every third day, no clothes but shorts and a T-shirt, sleep on the floor).

Eventually he stopped fighting, but served five years anyway, developing a new opinion of himself. "I didn't like what I was becoming. I'm still not comfortable with me." By the time of his release at the age of twenty-two, he trusted almost no one.

With all the changes that have occurred in him since then, Sy does not say that prison made him what he is: only that it helped. After completing the first five-year term, he took a job in Rochester working for a company that makes tanks for chemicals. He fell in love, got married, had three children. Between them, he and his wife were making close to $16,000 a year; quite enough at the time. Still, he was moody, depressed. One night when his two-year-old daughter would not stop crying, he reached for a six-pack. He recalls, horrified, that he was about to fling it at her, and glances sheepishly at the photograph of smiling Alicia, now eighteen, on the cell wall. "The problem wasn't the family. It was me. The things that were in my: anger, bitterness, a lack of understanding. I don't want to get, you know, into a highly philosophical or psychological thing; but there was confusion that was not there before." (He uses "you know" when he is about to say something that does not appeal to him.) He pauses. "One day I started, you know, robbing people."

"What were you thinking when you pointed a gun at someone whose money you didn't even need?"

"I wasn't thinking. I was just acting out feelings."

"Why pick robbery?"

"I don't know. It could have been murder."

"Were you getting back at people?"

"No. I had become more *like* people." He shifts his weight on the cot and looks both certain and surprised.

For armed robbery, and because he was a two-time felony

offender, they gave Sy fifteen to thirty years, of which he served eleven. During that time his wife divorced him.

At Stormville he got on the wrong side of the "keepers" for speaking his mind, he contends. "This was in '71, when Attica jumped off." The reminder is suddenly chilling in this place. "They said I was trying to change people's ideas. I think that any man who sees the truth is obligated to share that truth. That's what I was doing." For the effort, he says, he was handcuffed behind his back and "thrown down a couple of flights of stairs, you know. They fractured my eardrum. They fractured my left cheekbone."

He is interrupted by a rapid banging on the cell wall. He yells: "Maestro, I'm busy right now!" His neighbor, Maestro, is so called because he plays the guitar. No, Maestro is not his friend. Sy has no friends. The worst time of day for him is when he is let out of his cell. He finds prison life too dangerous, too unpredictable. He, who would deem it dishonorable to steal from a fellow inmate, has already had a watch and a pocket calculator stolen. He mentions this twice, angrily, in the course of two hours. "In my cell," he says, "I only have to worry about myself."

In his cell he can also do the reading he seems to need. Having recently finished *Wuthering Heights,* he concludes that "Heathcliff was one of the book's lesser villains" and that "he wasn't as strong as he appeared to be. The real Heathcliff only came through at the end." Then, with curiosity: "When Heathcliff was himself, no one understood him any more." Of Jean Valjean in *Les Misérables* Sy observes, "Any time you make a person into something other than himself, you make a monster."

He has read almost all of Richard Wright, even *The Outsider,* Wright's existential novel about a criminal who seeks to get outside everything, including morality and history.

To Sy this is impossible: "You can only become so much of an outsider." One is obliged to live in the world, although "you've got to walk up your own staircase, not someone else's."

Moreover, Wright, like Brontë and Hugo, was portraying a hero who was partly the victim of others, and partly of himself. When Sy says, "I want to understand whether I was the sole cause of what has happened to me," his expression is earnest to the point of desperation.

On the poem "Invictus," he says he does not believe he is "the master of my fate." The poem is on the wall because such a thing represents a goal. Sy wrote a poem himself, at the age of eighteen, when he was in Comstock. He recites it too rapidly:

> *Reminiscing my childhood past*
> *Of the good and the bad*
> *The happy and the sad*
> *The wasted tears and future fears*
> *That all came true.*

In spite of the accuracy of the poem's forecast, Sy is still bewildered by his latest crime. He is now doing six to twelve years for the attempted murder of his "lady" in Poughkeepsie. After serving time for the robbery conviction, he began to work with delinquent teenagers, but he got into trouble there, too, fighting with the authorities over their rough handling of the kids. "They told me: Everybody does it. I told them: *I* don't do it. *I'm* part of everybody." He lost that job and "drank and drank." Then he lost his lady, and one day he went after her where she worked—just had to talk, he says. Nonetheless, he had a shotgun with him that went off in a scuffle with the wom-

179

an's fellow employees. She was wounded. Sy didn't mean it. No, he does not see a parallel between this crime and his first trouble: pursuing a girlfriend and winding up in prison. "This time I was responsible." The thought does not console him.

Still, what clearly worries him more than the shooting incident is the recollection of how afraid of him the woman was. With her he had tried to make a whole life within a family of two, in a sense, as he describes it, to protect himself by building a cell on the outside. "But my lady couldn't adhere to my philosophy because she had nothing to base it on. My foundation was crumbling. I thought: Here it is, inside my unit." The "it" is threatening but unidentified. He used to say to her: "The reason I love you is that you like the good side of me. But there is something else, and this I don't want you to see." Until the afternoon of the shooting, he had managed to stay out of jail for three and a half years.

"So here I was in the grinder again. I knew what I had to face. You get into the machine and you're just a little cog. You're nothing major." An eerie falsetto fills the corridor. An inmate walks by outside the door to Sy's cell, shouting for his ID.

"Who are you now?"

"I don't really think about myself. I don't like myself, per se, because the things I have gone through have become such a part of me." As ever, there is no touch of self-pity in his voice. He seems to regard his life scientifically, like an unknown substance. I was thrown into a place where I couldn't develop normally," he says, quickly surveying his surroundings.

Does he think he will do something to put himself back in prison after this sentence is served? He feels that he has learned to moderate his expectations; that, he says, will help. Yet his resolution continues to be undermined by his temper. Even now he is on disciplinary report for raising his hand to a guard. He demonstrates the gesture as if to denote its casual innocence, but in fact a flick of his wrist is menacing. "I will always be in prison," he says after awhile. "It was something stamped on my soul."

What are prisons for, Sy? Punishment mainly, he believes, of four distinct types. The first one is one's loss of freedom. The second, the loss of a sense of responsibility: "You're expected to think for yourself and at the same time to follow orders without asking questions." The third kind of punishment he calls "sensory deprivation," the forced absence of family, of feeling. The only emotions one knows in prison, he says, are the "negatives" of anger and disappointment. And the fourth type? That, to Sy, is the most severe. "The worst punishment is being compelled to be someone other than yourself."

To see Sy Jackson from the inside is to agree that, in part, he has been compelled to be someone else. To see him from the outside, from the other end of his cot, is to acknowledge that the man is an explosive, someone to be afraid of. With that view Sy would wholeheartedly sympathize; he is afraid of himself. If the prisons in which he has spent nearly half his life have provided various punishments, they have also given him a context for looking into his own mind. Since what frightens him about his mind was nurtured in prison, the process of self-examination is as circular and enclosed as Sy's upstate odyssey. Such nonprogress may be typical of a great many prisoners, but as one discovers in a place like Attica, no inmate is typical. All the instruments of uniformity in a prison—the architecture, the outfits, the language, and routine—merely emphasize the fact that here, as elsewhere, every cell contains a person.

What disturbs anyone looking at Sy, however, is not his differences from the world but his obvious membership in it. In a sense a criminal is merely a man of extremes, someone who robs gas stations rather than the dignity of a colleague, or who terrorizes with a gun rather than a bullying personality, or who murders in fact instead of with gossip. Perhaps this is why Sy feels low but not ignoble; the laws he breaks are on the books. Yet his internal torment is that of anyone who recognizes his own guilt and self-hate, who sees in Sy's black-brown eyes all the imprisonment of the species. It is doubtful that Sy realizes this. One thing a prison does naturally is to ostracize its residents, most of whom are bound to think there is no one in the outer world remotely like them.

Sy had a dream while taking a nap the other day. It was about "a big, gigantic bird without feathers, and he came into my cell and got lodged under my cot. And I'm wondering in my dream whether to free this monster or scream for help." The problem struck him as funny. He did not recognize the beast.

{ essay in *Time* magazine }

From the Memoir
Kayak Morning

O bjects I never intended to see take on dispropor-
tionate significance. The gull's stone eye. The heron's wobbly legs. A jellyfish suspended like an
open parachute just below the surface of the water, the red
veins in the chute. A tassel of seaweed attached to a log.
And the log itself, blackened, drifting toward my kayak. It
looks like a swimming dog. I cannot tell if I am seeing the
whole thing or a portion of it. I wallop the waves. The log
creates a weir. I swerve in one direction. The log swerves
in another, as if it were steering on its own. See? It edits
itself. The creek is a palimpsest lined with corrections.

Kayaking is like writing, requiring the same precision
and restraint. You are definite, stabbing the paddle blades
into the water. Wild swings will get you nowhere. Writing requires generosity toward every point of view—the
water's point of view, and that of the birds and of the sky,
and of the algae, and of the insects. Writing is for important things, matters of substance. There is no point in going
out in a kayak unless you feel the potential profundity of
the act, the adventure that opens before you. You are alone,
and not alone. No one writes alone. Write, and you are in
the company of all who have written before you. No one
paddles alone.

From the Unpublished Memoir
Unaccompanied Minor

Mr. Chevigny is furious at me. I am ten, and I have left my bike on its side near the entrance to number 34. Wizard did not pull him away in time, and Mr. Chevigny nearly tripped over the bike. He speaks in a loud grumble, never with pleasantries, and he seems angry enough ordinarily, without a careless kid placing impediments in his path. I'm sorry, Mr. Chevigny. He growls. Aggh! Tall and bony, he holds tight to Wizard's leash, and follows the German Shepherd up the stone steps to his apartment house.

I wonder how it is to be blind, especially for Mr. Chevigny, who was not blind from birth. When he was not yet forty, he was diagnosed with a detached retina in one eye, and soon went blind in both. For more than half his life, then, he could see. Small wonder he was so angry. Small wonder, too, that besides the *Mr. and Mrs. North* radio series, he wrote *The Shadow*—the spooky crime fighter who had the power to cloud men's minds so that they could not see him.

When I was in college, I asked if I might come and visit Mr. Chevigny and talk about writing. He was very welcoming. I got the impression it was unusual for him to do that sort of thing. He spoke of the peculiar difficulties of writing for radio, transitions particularly, and how hard it is for characters to deliver information that does not come off as stilted or contrived. On one episode of *The Shadow,*

Lamont Cranston tells his companion, Well, Margot, here it is the next day.

I made an awkward remark about how trying it must be to make one's way in the world without being able to see. It's not a liability when you write for the radio, he said, and smiled briefly.

And there's something else of value in being blind. When you're blind, Roger, you know the location of things only in relation to other things. I moved around my library fluidly because I know where the end table is, thus I know where my writing desk is, thus I know where the book stand is where I keep my Braille dictionary. Everything leads me to something else. Blind people are acutely aware of sequences, more than sighted people, I think. You want to be a writer? Pay attention to what leads to what.

Spark's Other Notes

The Great Gatsby

If you hold *The Great Gatsby* upside down and shake it hard enough, the only real human being who falls out is Wilson the garage man. Gatsby is obsessed to the point of madness. Daisy is a dangerous nitwit. Tom is a thug, Jordan a crook, Meyer (though decent), a gangster. Even Nick, for all his moralizing, is mere talk, and not even that when it counts. Only the poor deceived Wilson is identifiable as one of us suffering slobs. So what is Fitzgerald saying by this—that one does not make memorable fiction out of ordinary suffering slobs? That no one would read *The Great Wilson?* I think so.

Dr. Jekyll and Mr. Hyde

It has to be about drugs. Jekyll is a junkie. Right?

Ulysses

Everyone who followed Homer minced words about *Ulysses,* including Dante. All of them pussy-footed around the story, which seems to me to be as plain as daylight. What made Ulysses's eye rove, along with the rest of him, was the irresistible attraction of doing the wrong thing—of doing it again and again, and knowing that he was doing the wrong thing. It shows what a good man Dante was that he could not bring himself to say that outright.

The Secret Agent

There's a scene in Conrad's novel that merely appears to be part of the plot, but I think it explains everything one needs to know about Verloc, the anarchist. Verloc is lying on the couch. His wife is in the kitchen. She has just figured out that he is responsible for the death-by-bomb of her young son. She gets a kitchen knife and heads for Verloc. Conrad describes the scene by telling us that Verloc has time to see her in the kitchen, time to see her get the knife, and time to see her walk toward him; but he does not have time to do anything about it. That's Verloc, and all anarchists. Their timing is off.

Sir Gawain and the Green Knight, "Kubla Khan," *A Christmas Carol, Moby-Dick, The Maltese Falcon, For Whom the Bell Tolls, Remembrance of Things Past* (all eight books), *The Waste Land,* "September 1, 1939," and *Hamlet*

All these works have their moments, but not one of them makes an ounce of sense. Especially *Hamlet.* For God's sake, *Goldilocks and the Three Bears* makes more sense than *Hamlet.* I just wanted to get that off my chest.

De Bello Gallico

Every first-year Latin student learns from Julius Caesar that "all Gaul is divided into three parts." Well, well! That's a relief!

King Lear

It's stupendous, of course. But didn't Lear notice some difference in his daughters' characters *before* he divvied up the kingdom?

The Prophet

Sophisticates like to make fun of Kahlil Gibran's *The Prophet.* I don't know why.

Here, for example, is a typical passage: "Almustafa, the chosen and the beloved, who was a dawn until his own day, had waited twelve years in the city of Orphalese for his ship that was to return and bear him back to the isle of his birth. And in the twelfth year, on the seventh day of

Ielool, the month of the reaping, he climbed the hill without the city walls and looked seaward." What's wrong with that, I'd like to know?

The Bible

From John 3:8: "The wind bloweth where it listeth." Excuse me?

Pope

Alexander Pope, the proudest, not to say touchiest of men, wrote: "Thus, let me love, unseen, unknown; thus unlamented let me die; steal from the world, and not a stone tell where I lie." The stone would have been unnecessary. Here's where he lied.

Shakespeare

If you wish to impress your friends, you can interrupt them every time they unknowingly quote Shakespeare. Here's a sampler: "The dog of war"; "a charmed life"; "yeoman's service"; "thereby hangs the tale"; "foul play"; "melted . . . into thin air"; "cold comfort"; "my mind's eye"; "for ever and a day"; "one fell swoop"; and "lay on, Macduff"—for which one has to know someone named Macduff.

Wordsworth

Better than you think. A lot better, actually.

Tocqueville and Dr. Johnson

Even though it is de rigueur to quote either or both of these men in any speech or article, they were not the same person. Johnson, particularly, has been misrepresented in history, mainly because Boswell was easily amused, and so he played up the wise-guy in Johnson—"Sir," this and "Sir," that, followed by what passed for a zinger in eighteenth-century London. The real Dr. Johnson was an unattractive, tormented man who had a psychotic fear of death and, yet, showed a magnificent affinity for the underclass,

of which he was one. If you want to quote the real Johnson, try this: "The test of civilization is how it treats its
poor."

Kafka's The Metamorphosis
Probably about a hangover, but still mesmerizing.

{ from the essay collection *Anything Can Happen* }

189

A Christmas Carol

Dickens made us think that the third ghost did the trick, but I believe it was the first. Naturally Scrooge was terrified by the image of his future death, just as he was mortified by the promise of its anonymity; and the prognosis of Tiny Tim undoubtedly touched his heart. Still, what really turned the tide, I think, was the first vision conjured by the Ghost of Christmas Past, the one of Scrooge as a boy sitting at his desk in the near-deserted school at Christmastime. That was Scrooge as we'd hardly known him, as he hardly knew himself, no less lonely than the man he grew into, and certainly no happier; only young.

Christmas Past is the least picturesque of Dickens's spirits. It has none of the fierce boisterousness of the Ghost of Christmas Present, none of the gray dreadfulness of the Ghost of Christmas Yet to Come. A prosaic bear-but-a-touch-of-my-hand ghost, it displays its episodes to Scrooge like a conventional historian, altering nothing, almost never stating the morals of the tales, or recriminations. The past has already happened, so what can a guide say but "there"? And it's a gentle ghost, besides; it doesn't overact like Marley.

Nevertheless it is "a strange figure" that parts Scrooge's bed curtains: "like a child; yet not so like a child as like an old man, viewed through some supernatural medium, which gave him the appearance of having receded from the view, and being diminished to a child's proportions." The ghost embodies time. It knows, as Scrooge learns, that the past is as mysterious as the future, just as out of reach, as imprecise and malleable as the present, and as likely to be falsely seen or spoken for. The past is as wide open as the future, too.

When the ghost shows young Scrooge to the old, it has had to choose carefully. All that immense and jumbled time in the old man's life, but only certain things will affect him.

The boy at the desk is the first thing Scrooge sees on his journey, and he is immediately moved to tears.

Of course the sight of oneself as a child is grossly sentimental. Dickens-haters love to trample such scenes and repeat Oscar Wilde's observation that anyone who would not laugh at the death of Little Nell must indeed have a heart of stone. A hurt and lonely child is hard enough to bear, much less when that child is you, before the fall. You want back everything you were, and there you are: able to be hurt, unable to hurt back, unencumbered by your own ill will. As superintendent of such scenes, the Ghost of Christmas Past doesn't need to hoot and holler; there's terror enough in the act—to hurl back all those years and be the future gaping at the past as if it were bright as the future.

This is happening in Scrooge's mind: both the boy at school, and Scrooge looking at the boy. The man reaches for the child and vice versa, though they are reaching for two different things—Scrooge wishing to be young, but not lonely; the child wanting to be old, but not Scrooge. Neither will have it his way, yet Scrooge weeps "to see his poor forgotten self as it used to be." Why? Does he really seek to recover all that punishing innocence?

Perhaps he sees something else in his past, something other than young Scrooge, that he wants back. It could be his imagination, so long held in check, but which, as he recalls, ran wild as a boy. Maybe his imagination is coming back to him tonight for a fling on Christmas Eve—unless you really believe in ghosts. Any mind that could fancy such a journey as Scrooge's can't be all gone. And Scrooge is not hopeless, after all. He has been caricatured by time, but looked at coldly, he is merely a bony Republican—not an honorable calling, but no devil either. Perhaps it is the past itself that reduces Scrooge to tears.

After the visitations, Scrooge swears that from now on he will live in the past, present, and future, thus giving equal consideration to each ghost. But in fact Scrooge has always lived in the present and future, essential for "a good man of business"; it was the past that he had neglected, and the dead. "Old Marley was as dead as a doornail," Dickens tells us in the first paragraph of the story. But how dead is a doornail? As dead as a door knocker, that's for sure, yet the knocker on Scrooge's door is alive with Marley, and Marley with it. "The wisdom of our ancestors is in the simile," says Dickens. Exactly.

Dickens goes to some lengths to remind us that Marley is dead: "this must be distinctly understood, or nothing wonderful can come of the story." It must be distinctly understood that time past is time present, as Eliot's confused narrator says in *Four Quartets,* that all time is both "eternally present" and "unredeemable." Hamlet must meet his ghost, Scrooge his. Scrooge's nephew tells him that "we are all fellow-passengers to the grave," but occupants of the grave make passage too. Marley fairly shrieks at Scrooge to believe in him.

Marley, as Dickens says straight out, is the key to

Scrooge's salvation. The chain he drags has the gift of metaphor; a chain is ponderous when it stands for worldly selfishness, but a chain may also link man to man, man to boy, and the past to the present and future.

What do you want with me, Scrooge asks Marley, who answers, "Much." What Marley and Dickens want of Scrooge is nothing short of the awareness of eternity.

The sense of his place in time makes Scrooge weep—more than the sight of his lonely boyhood or the memory of his lost imagination. The boy in school achieves an epiphany in Scrooge's tears because he is not merely the image of one man as one child, but of all mankind deserted. When a connection is made, when Scrooge's sister Fan says that Ebenezer is welcome to come home for Christmas, that he has a home to come to, and a father, Scrooge weeps more deeply. This is the real mystery brought by the Ghost of Christmas Past—that life is bound to life, and that there is a natural order in which a strong life may tend toward a weak one, as Scrooge will finally tend toward Tiny Tim.

So Scrooge goes back in order to go forward, and when finally he goes forward, he goes back, behaving "as a schoolboy" when he discovers on Christmas morning that it is not too late to act on his repentance, that "the Time before him was his own." He says, "I'm quite a baby . . . I'd rather be a baby," which is proper in a season made for children. Then he walks around the city patting heads and questioning beggars, like Marley's ghost "abroad among his fellowmen."

He enjoys Christmas present, and we are assured that from now on he will know how "to keep Christmas well." To keep it is to preserve it as one does the past, not as in a museum case but as it really is—a state of consciousness no deader than a doornail. He knows that for Christmas to be kept in the present, it must be remembered, and when it is remembered as a time of going from loneliness to comfort, of the sudden and necessary revelation of our humanity, then it will be kept well. In time present, Scrooge the munificent strolls through London feeding the hungry and curing the lame. But he also still huddles at his school desk, waiting for a relative to take him home. Eventually he will learn that he is that relative, and weep for the life we share.

{ column in *The New Republic* }

Do Not Go for Cyrano's Nose

A particularly satisfying scene in *Cyrano de Bergerac* occurs when a lout seeks to attack the hero by making fun of his monumental nose. Cyrano waits patiently as the lout delivers some obvious and pathetic insults. Then, instead of running him through with his sword, which he is quite capable of doing, he steps forward to present his own list of insults to his nose, all of which are brilliant and funny; and while they appear to be self-deprecating, they actually constitute a devastating mockery of the lout's intelligence—an attack far more effective than anything the lout ever could have devised.

If one really wants to bring someone low, attack his or her ideas of opinions and not the person. Do it coldly and without a hem of passion showing. Also, be honest with one's criticism; do not distort the attackee's meaning by elliptical quotations or by false selections. Be occasionally magnanimous as well, even if disingenuously. One must remember that in an attack, the attacker is no less on display than the attackee. The result one seeks is to have people conclude that a scoundrel has been assaulted by a nobleman, not the reverse.

The one group I know of that has never learned this rule of sticking to the matter and not the person is writers. And, in this regard, they offer a useful example of how not to attack—and how not to live. As I write this entry, in fact, a typical and typically pointless literary battle is underway. John Irving has just attacked Tom Wolfe as being unreadable. Wolfe responded by attacking Irving as being washed-up as a novelist, along with Norman Mailer and John Updike, who had attacked Wolfe earlier. So it has always gone. Truman Capote on Jack Kerouac: "That's not writing. It's typing." Gore Vidal on Capote: "He has made lying an art. A minor art." The novelist James Gould Cozzens, perhaps professing sour grapes of wrath: "I cannot read ten pages of Steinbeck without throwing up."

Jazz musicians say only the most adoring things about one another; actors, generally the same. Only writers claw and spit, even though nobody cares but other writers, and public opinion of the attackee is affected not at all.

Yet here is H. L. Mencken's generous assessment of Henry James: "An idiot and a Boston idiot to boot, than which there is nothing lower in the world." And William Allen White's gracious description of Mencken: "With a pig's eye that never looks up, with a pig's snout that loves muck, with a pig's brain that knows only the sty, and a pig's squeal that cries only when he is hurt, he sometimes opens his pig's mouth, tusked and ugly, and lets out the voice of God, railing at the whitewash that covers the manure about his habitat." Small attack big, big attack small.

One trouble with the genre of insult is that it makes for wasteful digressions in a writer's career and is the antithesis of real, worthy writing itself. The aim of real writing is to make lives larger, more alert, and, with luck, happier. Attack writing is personal and seeks to do personal injury; it shrivels up everything it touches, by going for the nose.

It is also, by nature and intention, unfair and incomplete and frequently irrational.

Macaulay said of Socrates, "The more I read him, the

less I wonder that they poisoned him"—which might have made sense if Socrates (whom we know only from Plato) had left anything to read. Charles Kingsley called Shelley "a lewd vegetarian"—an intriguing idea but difficult to picture.

And it creates a false sense of accomplishment. Friends of an attacker will always rush to congratulate him on the meanness of his attack, because they get a two-fer: One writer has been belittled, and another has looked like a jackass doing it.

All enmity is personal, but it must not be made to sound that way. During a performance of Sheridan's *The Rivals,* the actor playing Sir Lucius O'Trigger was suddenly hit by an apple thrown by someone in the audience. "By the powers," he exclaimed. "Is it me, or the matter?" Always make it the matter.

{ from the instruction book *Rules for Aging* }

Would You Mind If
I Borrowed This Book?

Never lend books, for no one ever returns them:
the only books I have in my library are books
that other folks have lent me.
—Anatole France

O f all the terrifying assaults to which a writer's home is vulnerable, nothing equals that of a guest who stares straight at one's bookshelves. It is not the judgmental possibility that is frightening, the fact that one's sense of discrimination is exposed by his books. Indeed, most people would much prefer to see the guest first scan, then peer and turn away in boredom or disapproval. Alas, too often the eyes, dark with calculation, shift from title to title like a lecher in an overheated dance hall. And that is not the worst. It is when those eyes stop moving that the heart, too, stops. The guest's body twitches; his hand floats up to where his eyes have led it. There is nothing to be done. You freeze. He smiles. You hear the question even as it forms. "Would you mind if I borrowed this book?"

(Mind? Why should I mind? The fact that I came upon that book in a Paris bookstall in April 1959—the thirteenth I believe it was, the afternoon, it was drizzling. That I found it after searching all Europe and North America for a copy. That it is dog-eared at passages that mean more to my life than my heartbeat. That the mere touch of its pages recalls to me in a Proustian shower my first love, my best dreams. Should I mind that you seek to take all that away? That I will undoubtedly never get it back? Then even if you actually return it to me one day, I will be wizened, you cavalier, and the book soiled and spoiled by your mishandling? *Mind?*)

"Not at all. Hope you enjoy it."

"Thanks. I'll bring it back next week."

"No rush. Take your time. (Liar.)"

Not that there is any known way to avoid these exchanges. One has books; one has friends; they are bound to meet. Charles Lamb, who rarely railed, waxed livid on the subject: "Your borrowers of books—those mutilators of collections, spoilers of the symmetry of shelves, and creators of odd volumes." But how are such people to be put off, since *they* are often *we,* and the nonreturn of borrowed books is a custom as old as books themselves? ("Say, Gutenberg, what's *this?* And may I borrow it?") It is said that Charles I clutched a Bible as he mounted the scaffold. One shudders to imagine the last earthly question he heard.

Still, this custom confutes natures. In every other such situation, the borrower becomes a slave to the lender, the social weight of the debt so altering the balance of a relationship that a temporary acquisition turns into a permanent loss. This is certainly true with money. Yet it is not at all true with books. For some reason a book borrower feels that a book, once taken, is his own. This removes both memory and guilt from the transaction. Making matters worse, the lender believes it too. To keep up appearances, he may solemnly extract an oath that the book be brought back as soon as possible; the borrower answering with matching solemnity that the Lord might seize his eyes were he to do otherwise. But it is all a play. Once gone, the book is gone forever. The lender, fearing rudeness, never asks for it again. The borrower never stoops to raise the subject.

Can the borrowers be thwarted? There are attempts. Some hopefuls glue ex libris stickers to the inside covers (clever drawings of animals wearing glasses, and so forth)—as if the presence of Latin and the imprint of a name were so formidable as to reverse a motor reflex. It never works. One might try slipping false jackets on one's books—a cover for *The Secret Agent* disguising *Utility Rates in Ottawa: A Woman's View*. But book borrowers are merely despicable, not stupid. They tend to leaf before they pluck. Besides, the interesting thing about the feeling of loss when a book is borrowed is that the book's quality rarely matters. So mysterious is the power of books in our lives that every loss is a serious loss, every hole in the shelf a crater.

And this, of course, is the key to the sense of hopelessness in this matter. Our books are ourselves, our characters, our insulation against those very people who would take away our books. There, on that wall, Ahab storms. Hamlet mulls. Molly Bloom says yes yes yes. Keats looks into Chapman, who looks at Homer, who looks at Keats. All this happens in a bookshelf continually—while you are out walking the dog, or pouting, or asleep. The Punic Wars rage, Emma Bovary pines; Bacon exhorts others to behave the way he never could. Here French is spoken. There Freud. So go war and peace, pride and prejudice, decline and fall, perpetually in motions as sweeping as Milton's or as slight as Emily Dickinson contemplating the grass.

These things are not what we have, but what we are.

Leigh Hunt exulted: "Nothing can deprive me of my value for such treasures. I can help the appreciation of them while I last, and love them till I die; and perhaps, if fortune turns her face in kindness upon me before I go, I may chance, some quiet day, to lay my over-beating temples on a book, and so have the death I most envy." Plato was reputedly found dead with a book under his pillow, Petrarch in his library with his elbow resting on an open page. Books gave them more than solace. They were their lives extended, a way of touching eternity.

Why else, then, would writers do almost everything for books, to acquire and preserve them, to prevent their banning or burning? Stories of manuscripts lost or destroyed are especially heartbreaking because one knows how ephemeral ideas and images are, what vast effort it takes to dust off the confusions, tune out the noise, and create those books that, for whatever inadequacies they may display, still set the mind in order for a time, giving it a spine and a binding. There may be no more pleasing picture in the world than that of a child peering into a book—the past and the future entrancing each other. Neither does anyone look quite so attractive as with a book in hand. How many people have fallen in love merely at the sight of someone reading?

All of which would appear to offer an argument that booklending ought to be encouraged. It is the supreme selfless act, after all. Should we not abjure our pettiness, open our libraries, and let our most valued possessions fly from house to house, sharing the wealth? Certain clerics with vows of poverty did this. Inside their books was printed not ex libris but ad usum—for the use of—indicating that it is better to lend than to keep, that all life's gifts are transitory. Should we not follow the clerics? Or might we just for once summon our true feelings on this subject and, upon hearing the terrible questions, smile back and speak from the heart: "Mind? I'll break your *arm*, you bastard!"

{ essay in *Time* magazine }

Life in the Margins

Once I borrowed a book of essays called *The Immediate Experience,* by the cultural critic Robert Warshow WHO HE? from an old and learned friend. HE'S LEARNED, SO YOU'RE LEARNED? My friend had so thoroughly marked up the text that his annotations constituted a parallel text of its own, consisting of his annoyances, approvals, elaborations, questions, and challenges—so?

Some passages were underlined in black ink, some in blue magic marker, some in green, some in thick red. There were solid red and green arrows pointing from one paragraph to another. RED AND GREEN = STOP AND GO? There were equal signs followed by pithy interpretations. PITHY YET! Words such as *key* and *why?* were written alongside certain sentences. YES, YES, GET TO IT! I had borrowed one book and was reading two. INTERESTING—MAYBE.

The subject AS IF WE HADN'T GUESSED is marginalia— the notes one makes in response to something, usually in books. A forthcoming book called *Marginalia* WHAT ELSE?, by H. J. Jackson (Yale University Press), deals exclusively with the marginalia in books, but it also suggests the wider subject of how the mind works generally.

Every thought breeds an internal commentary, a counterthought NOT ALWAYS, some elaboration on the initial matter. Every action taken incurs an inner comment.

EVERY ACTION? Everything we are is under continual

revision. We even live in the margins of one another's lives. PROVE IT! In a sense, Boswell was the marginalia to Dr. Johnson's life, which would not have been celebrated had there been no work in the margins. DIDN'T J. HAVE A LIFE WITHOUT B.?

But the major premise of marginalia is that life is infinitely adjustable. As soon as a work comes under someone else's scrutiny, up rises the impulse to correct, enlarge, destroy. One might go so far as to say marginalia reveal the human desire not to accept finality. BE CAREFUL! The idea of ghosts, or heaven, may be our marginalia on death. GIVE ME A BREAK! It was interesting to learn from Jackson's book TO WHICH THIS ESSAY IS MARGINALIA, I SUPPOSE, that friends would deliberately lend Coleridge their books, knowing he would mark them up endlessly. Thus, the lenders would be getting back a book improved by Coleridge.

Other writers known for their relentless annotations were Horace Walpole, Charles Darwin, Thomas Macaulay, and William Blake. I LOVE BLAKE. But quality that high is rare. We take a book out of the library and read the marginalia, often surly and stupid, of anonymous strangers. THANKS A HEAP! The fun, though, is to respond to them, by which we perpetuate the argument and extend the text. BACK TO HIS THESIS, AT LAST? Or, one can simply respond to the language and doodle: thesis, Croesus, Jesus. JESUS!

And this practice goes way beyond reading. I sit and watch some political commentator on television and write in the margins of the air. DOES ANYONE KNOW WHAT'S GOING ON IN THIS COUNTRY? An acquaintance slithers into some self-aggrandizing prevarication. I air-write, LIAR! A nice, honest moment occurs in the new, good movie *Traffic* when the US drug czar, Michael Douglas, falters in the middle of a false and insincere speech, and you can see his conscience writing marginalia on his claptrap.

Marginalia create the presence of more than one voice at a time SEE COMPUTER MESSAGES, and this cacophony simulates the ways our minds work. The difference between thought and speech—the inchoate mess in our minds as opposed to the crispy words that emerge—suggests that we live with a number of voices at once. SPOOKY! If we really wanted to get spooky about it, we might wonder how to tell the texts of our lives from the margins. What I am writing at this moment may be the marginalia to feelings of loss and pain that do not appear in the sentence. The feelings of loss and pain may constitute the text of my life for which all sentences, written or spoken, create a defense or rebuke.

The point AT LAST is that whatever is put in the margins in some way enhances the center by deflating certainty and that this infinite operation makes up who we are. For example, I may have got everything in this essay all wrong. NO KIDDING! I may have got my life all wrong. DON'T MAKE ME CRY! And so I may have to start all over again and fill up the margins YOU'RE RUNNING OUT OF SPACE until I run out of space.

{ essay in *Time* magazine }

From the Memoir
The Boy Detective

I sound as though I read a lot as a boy, but, except for detective fiction, I didn't. More book-storeish than bookish, I often took my pursuits to the Fourth Avenue bookstores between Ninth and Fourteenth Streets. Caves on a boulevard, where the antique books, like shelves of rocks, extended deep into mists. If there had been any order to the inventory, it was buried in the minds of the proprietors, old Commies mainly, who rarely looked up from whatever manifesto they were reading. Each one sat monklike in the front of his shop, by the door, and raised and eyelid or two as you entered. A kid, even a detective, would receive no notice. It hardly mattered. My business was not with the old men, but rather with the books— black, brown, maroon. The sweet-dust smell. The dates of old publications. I bought a biography of Napoleon written in the 1880s, and the essays of Macaulay, and short stories by Jack London. Everything dirt cheap.

I can't remember ever reading any of them. What I sought from the books was a connection to past mysteries. In the best detective stories, something terrible that happened long ago erupts in a crime of the present. I would nose around one store after another (there were at least twenty-five of them), as if I were hunting for something specific. The proprietors never questioned my motives. They understood what I wanted. It was the same thing they'd have wanted when they had relocated their lives to the bookstore. Quiet, strange, dark. No money in it for them. Eventually they moved to Florida.

Two bookstores are left in the area these days. The Alabastar, between Eleventh and Twelfth Streets, is not one of the originals, as it was established in 1996. But it has the look and feel of the great old stores. The Strand, founded in 1927, has hung on all these years, among the newer enterprises of art supply centers, low-rise apartments, and stores that sell Halloween costumes and "fantasy apparel." Everything looks alike, but so did the old bookstores. They just looked better, alike. A friend of my son John's works in the Strand. He reports whenever a book of mine winds up in the one-dollar bin. "Overpriced," he says. I go to the Strand from time to time, but today it's a little too café and eager to please, for my taste. I think it feels abandoned. I think it misses the companionship of the other stores. I try to picture the day they went out of business. A truck pulls up out front. The books are carried out like patients from a nursing home. And for a moment, before demolition, the obvious vacant walls.

From the Unpublished Memoir
Unaccompanied Minor

I am thirteen. In one of the Fourth Avenue bookstores, I dig out a small collection by Patrick Kavanagh. Standing in the near blackness of the store's catacombs, I open the book at random to the poem, "Wet Evening in April":

> The birds sang in the wet trees
> And I listened to them. It was a hundred years from now
> And I was dead and someone else was listening to them
> But I was glad I had recorded for him
> The melancholy.

Are all poems elegies? Something is gone. Or some place. Or someone. The relentless feeling of absence seems to gnaw at the minds of the poets. I learn the word *elegiac*. "Round Midnight" is elegiac. I think I may be elegiac myself, in my nature, I mean. Some day, I may write elegiac things, inventories of all one may miss in a life. The turn in the road. Years. Opportunities. People. Home.

A Teacher of Books

Douglas Bush died on March 2 (1983) at the age of eighty-six, after forty-six years as professor of English Literature at Harvard and a life of devotion to "Paradise Lost." The obituary in *The New York Times* made him out a gentle crank, quoting a complaint of Bush's that too many students attend universities these days, and thus cannot be adequately educated—the sort of hackneyed wail that Bush himself would never have dwelt on or even considered right plucked from a greater, kindlier context. Bush's world was the greater, kindlier context. Like Samuel Johnson, he knew everything worth knowing. Like Johnson, too, he was born to teach books. Few people are. It is an odd pursuit. Literary study stands at the center of modern education, and at the center of the writer's life, but when one tries to determine what happens in the relationship among book, student, and teacher, the teacher grows shadowy, eventually vanishes.

Of course, teachers of every subject suffer from obsolescence, that being almost a tool of the trade if one's students are to build on what they learn, even to the point of rejecting it at the onset of independent thinking. Good teachers yearn to be obliterated.

Good teachers of literature have little choice in the matter. The *Hamlet* they pry open for the nineteen-year-old will not be the *Hamlet* that student reads at age fifty. The play will have changed because the reader's experience will have recast it—the noble, tormented boy of one's youth reappearing in middle age as something of a drip.

But even at the moment that a teacher of literature is doing his job, the work is hard to put a name to. What precisely is it that you did, Professor Bush? Every teacher knows the boredom and terror of that question. A teacher of French teaches French, a teacher of piano, piano. But a teacher of Proust, Austen, Donne, Faulkner, Joyce? Are not the writers the teachers themselves? Oh, one can see the need for a tour guide now and then: notes, terms, some scraps of biography. But surely the great books were written for people, and if they require the presence of middlemen, then they could never have been so great in the first place. So goes the cant.

In point of plain fact, a teacher of literature may do several quite different things, especially these days when universities house their own schools of thought on the subject. Some teach the formal aspects of literature, some the sociology of literature, some the politics. Still, something central seems to be conveyed in the teaching of literature beyond a particular point of view, something in the attitude of the teacher toward both his students and the books: his concentration, his appreciation, occasionally his awe. Awe can be a powerful pedagogical instrument, the sight of someone overwhelmed overwhelming by refraction. True, the relationship of teacher to the work of art is that of a middleman, but in the best circumstances the middleman becomes a magnifying glass. ("Do you see *this*?") Instead of intruding between Yeats and his reader, he shows Yeats in the light, reveals not only poetry but how poetry comprehends the world, thus lending his students the eyes of the poet. At full strength, the teacher is an artist himself, and not just for restorations.

Treating the book as an event, he manipulates it the way the writer manipulated reality, making of literature what the writer made of life.

So what is it he does in that mysterious classroom when the thick wood door shuts behind him and the rows of too young faces turn and rise like heliotropic plants, eager for a sign? "Today we consider." Is that in fact what "we" are considering today? Or are we considering the teaching considering Kafka, and if that is the case, what exactly is to be considered—the learned scholar stocked deep with information about "irony" and "metaphor," or the still deeper mind, which has confronted Kafka alone in a private dark, and which Kafka has confronted in turn? "How does one say that (D. H.) Lawrence is right in his great rage against the modern emotions, unless one speaks from the intimacies of one's own feelings, and one's own sense of life, and one's own worked-for way of being?" asked Lionel Trilling. The testimony is always personal. Behind the spectacles and the fuzzy coat, the teacher teaches himself.

His faith in books cannot be easy to acquire. An English teacher must learn to live before becoming good at his work, since literature demands that one know a great deal about life—not to have settled life's problems, but at least to recognize and accept the wide, frail world in which those problems have a home. The achievement of such perspective involves a penalty, too. He who has gained that generous view inevitably moderates the books in his charge, domesticates their subversiveness, puts out the fire. As moderator he becomes a caricature, as teachers of English in fiction are always portrayed as caricatures. Who's afraid of Virginia Woolf's professor? The practice of giving apples to teachers may have originated as an unconscious mockery of their lack of experience and danger, of their apparent refusal to risk the loss of paradise.

And yet the power they generate can be enormous. Remember? One may not know exactly what happens in those classrooms, but one knows that it did happen, long after the fact, after all the classrooms and schools are left behind. Two, perhaps three, teachers in a lifetime stick in the mind, and one of them is almost always a teacher of literature. He remains not as presiding deity but as a person, someone impassioned about words on paper. Perhaps he knows that words are all we have, all that stand between ourselves and our destruction. The teacher also intervenes. Robert Hollander, Jr., of Princceton described a class of R. P. Blackmur's, who taught Hollander the Dante he now teaches to others: "The lecturer gasped, tottered, and finally settled ruinously into total silence. He stood there, I thought, debating whether or not to chuck it all up, leave the room (with twenty minutes still to run before the bell), perhaps even to leave the earth." Danger enough.

Courage too, of a sort. Who but a teacher of books dares claim as his province the entire range of human experience, intuition no less than fact? Who else has the nerve? And what does he do with this vast territory he has staked out for himself? He invites us in, says in effect there has never been anything written, thought, or felt that one need be afraid to confront. A teacher of books may favor this or that author or century, but fundamentally his work is the antithesis of prejudice. Take it all, he urges; the vicious with the gentle. Do not run from anything you can read. Above all, do not become enraged at what is difficult or oblique. You too are difficult, oblique, and equally worth the effort.

It may be that such people remain with it because they were always with it from the start. Basically the enterprise of teaching literature is a hopeful one, the hope residing with the upturned faces. First faith, then hope. If words are merely words after all, then the teacher of books may be the world's most optimistic creature. No matter how he may grumble about life's decay, it is he who, year after year, trudges up the stone steps of old, dank buildings, hauls himself before the future, and announces, against all reason of experience, that "the World was all before them."

With those words, Milton approached the end of his long moral poem, and when Douglas Bush came to read those words aloud before his Harvard classes, there was nothing in his voice that betrayed a personal reverberation to the grand dismay the words contain. Bush showed none of Blackmur's visible force or Trilling's visible elegance, though like them he believed in the good that words and people are capable of. On the last day of courses at Harvard, it is the custom for students to applaud the teachers they most appreciate. After years of suffering this embarrassment, Bush would begin to pack up his books in the last minutes of the hour, so that he could time his exit from the room right at the bell. Thus when the moment arrived, and Bush was already halfway down the steps, it appeared that the students were clapping on and on for someone not there. But he was there.

{ essay in *Time* magazine }

From the Unpublished Memoir
Unaccompanied Minor

As in illness, when one can no longer recall how it feels to be in good health, I fall into a depression without knowing what a depression is. All the strut and swagger of my early childhood seems like a story about someone else. I miss the power that child had, the urge and ability to wonder at everything outside oneself. Mr. Shank is a great help to me in this, because he does look at the world with wonder and pleasure. By remarks he makes in class, one knows he regularly goes to art galleries and to the theater. At one time in his life, he must have hoped to go into acting or directing, because he has a degree from the Yale Drama School. He teaches our class *Hamlet* by first having us build a model of the Globe Theater.

He sees a writer in me, and because he does, I begin to see one as well. He chooses me for a citywide literary competition. Kids recite poems before an audience, and judges pick the best presentation. I choose Auden's elegy to Yeats. Mr. Shank teaches me how to pronounce *quays*. I do not win the competition, but I feel a little important, included. For the first time in recent memory, I am happy to be included.

One Saturday, he invites me to his loft in a converted office building next to Lord & Taylor on Thirty-ninth Street, off Fifth. Everything seems exotic to me. Who has a home in a commercial district? Who lives in a loft? The place bubbles over with romantic strangeness—samovars and stone busts and framed prints and a four-poster bed with a black duvet, and one black wall. Mr. Shank has a partner named Richard, a blond, handsome man in his thirties whom Mr. Shank introduces to me as his roommate. I know nothing of homosexuality (I hardly know that much about heterosexuality), and nothing in their behavior makes me feel uncomfortable.

We play Scrabble, and it is clear from the outset that the game is a battlefield for the two men. With my comparatively meager vocabulary I finish a distant third, as Richard and Mr. Shank torment each other with words that may or may not exist. Mr. Shank, the cleverer of the two, loves to make up new words and when challenged, to invent absurd definitions for them. He earns a great many points for "kiddrawers," which he defines as pants for a baby goat. Then he laughs himself silly. There was no lover of language like Mr. Shank. Richard reports that the toilet bowl has a crack in it. Mr. Shank shoots back, "psycho-ceramic." When I leave their house, I feel I have been to someplace out of the Arabian nights, privileged to be surrounded by such intelligent splendor.

Years later, when I am in graduate school, I visit Mr. Shank again. He tells me that vandals broke into their apartment, took a dump on the bed, and scrawled fags and cocksuckers on the walls, in their own shit. He tells me this only with melancholy.

From the Memoir
The Boy Detective

I was aware of the world of writers at an early age. The faintest scent of brine. Then and now. But what should one expect? This is Twenty-sixth Street, where Herman Melville lived at number 104, embittered for nearly thirty years. By the time he moved into his dreary one-bedroom flat, he had already written *White-Jacket, Pierre,* and *Moby-Dick.* The critics had flogged him. He had no money. He survived by working as a customs inspector, a job he described as "worse than driving geese to water." Eventually he finished *Billy Budd* five months before he died, in 1891. The book was found among his papers, and was not published till 1924. No evidence of his house today. The lot is occupied by an office building next to the 69th Regiment Armory, a blackened Moby Dick of a building, where the Armory Show of modern American paintings was held in 1913, and where we neighborhood kids watched the New York Knicks in the early 1950s, before pro basketball got big.

Writers always have been drawn to the Gramercy Park area, which contained what Henry James, another resident, called "the incomparable tone of time." The park itself was a farm in the 1820s, bought by an entrepreneur, Samuel Ruggles, described as an advocate of open spaces, who spent $180,000 to drain the swamp on the property and create "Gramercy Square." This he deeded to the owners of forty-two parcels of land surrounding it. The park was enclosed by a fence in 1833, and a land-scaper, with the demanding name of James Virtue, planted trees and shrubs, as well as privet hedges inside the fence to enforce the border. Apparently, Ruggles's definition of open spaces was limited to two acres (.08 hectares) of elab-orately planned greenery and a gated Eden available only to those who lived directly around it and paid an annual fee for a key.

For myself, I could not stand the studied civility of the place—the perfect rectangular park; the staid and confi-dent benches; the birdhouses, like restored Machu Picchu temples, one at each end; the gravel pathways running among four lawns cut into the shape of piano tops—exclu-sive, average, tame. That, above all, was what depressed me about Gramercy Park, more than its will for pointless order and enclosure and its smug prettiness—the feeling that the neighborhood might foster and contain creativ-ity, but without the thrill of discovery, or self-discovery, or danger. Sea-level art. Gramercy Park seemed assured that it was better than anyone who lived there, with no evidence to support the assumption. Did Melville sense that as he walked these streets?

Yet the still, green neighborhood offered something for literary New York. Edith Wharton was born in a town house on the site of the Gramercy Park Hotel, now an apartment house on the north side of the park, in 1862. The sister poets, Phoebe and Alice Cary, moved here from Cincinnati in 1850, and established a literary salon that attracted such people as Horace Greeley, the editor of the *New York Tribune,* who advised young men to go west. Greeley had a three-story house at 35 East Nine-teenth Street, and kept goats in his backyard. Stephen Crane roomed with three artists, in a run-down building on Twenty-third Street, where he found a fitting quotation from Emerson chalked on a wall: "Congratulate yourself if you have done something strange and extravagant and broken the monotony of a decorous age." The National Arts Club, founded in 1898 on the south side of the park, included Mark Twain, W. H. Auden, and more recently, Frank McCourt among its members. E. B. White located Stuart Little in Gramercy Park. Hard to know if Stuart counts as a literary figure.

Williams Sydney Porter, O. Henry to his readers, lived a bit better than most of the area writers, at 55 Irving Place, because he had a steady job writing weekly stories for the *New York World* at $100 a pop. He spent most of his time hanging around Healy's Café across the street, and getting stinko with fellow writers, artists, and musicians. Healy's Café became Pete's Tavern, in which O. Henry was said to have written "The Gift of the Magi." During Prohibition, Pete's posed as a flower shop. Patrons walked past the cases of refrigerated flowers on their way to the bar. Summers, when we were in college, my wife, Ginny, and I would sit here at the outdoor tables, nurse beers, and speak of the life ahead of us. Tonight the tables are cold and white with frost.

Oscar Wilde lived at Seventeenth Street and Irving Place for a awhile. Minor literary figures, such as Carl Van Vechten and Paul Rosenfield lived on Irving Place as well. Local dinner parties were jazzed up by the likes of George Gershwin, F. Scott Fitzgerald, Theodore Dreiser, Ethel Barrymore, and Langston Hughes. They spilled gaily into what Van Vechten had called "the splendid drunken twenties." In 1927, Nathanael West took a position as night manager of the fleabag Kenmore Hotel on Twenty-third, where he wrote *The Day of the Locust* and snuck other writers into the hotel. Dashiell Hammett registered under the name Mr. T. Victoria Blueberry. West gave him the swankiest suite in the joint, where Hammett wrote *The Maltese Falcon*—telling of wicked women, murderers, and treasure three blocks from where Herman Melville, PI, alone and unnoticed, had tracked evildoers down the vast gray streets of the sea.

From the Unpublished Memoir
Unaccompanied Minor

I do not know what I'll write, but I know how I'll write. By ear. I will write by ear, the way I do everything else. Like Thelonius Monk, I will improvise. I will pay attention only to impulse. I will tell you this. I will tell you that. I will tell you something that happened a long time ago, and then something that happened yesterday, and then I'll tell you something that happened even before the first thing I told you. And I will trust you to take the scattered pieces as I present them, out of order, in hopes that you will be moved by their arranged disarrangement. I will write by ear, and you will read by ear. And we will play the tune together.

Call Us Ishmael

Here's literary relevance for you:

In the first chapter of *Moby-Dick,* called "Loomings," Ishmael considers why he chose to go on that momentous whaling voyage and concludes, half-kidding, that his decision must have been part of the "grand programme of Providence that was drawn up a long time ago." He calls his adventure "a sort of brief interlude and solo between more extensive performances" and sees the providential bill as having looked like this:

GRAND CONTESTED ELECTION FOR THE PRESIDENCY OF THE UNITED STATES

WHALING VOYAGE BY ONE ISHMAEL

BLOODY BATTLE IN AFGHANISTAN

The first headline is set in large, elegant type; the third, in bold, block type. The lettering of the middle event is small and plain, as if it were being whispered on the page.

And here we are, you and I—not about to undertake a whaling voyage, most likely, since whaling voyages are unusual and environmentally unpopular these days, but nonetheless about to undertake some small, private voyage of our own choosing, while around us, above and below, the more extensive performances of the world loom on: a grand contested election heating up (the 1980 presidential election), and some very bloody battles in Afghanistan (the Soviet attacks).

Melville chose Afghanistan because it has always seemed the most faraway place on earth, perhaps at times to the Afghans themselves. In 1851, when *Moby-Dick* was published, presidential elections must have seemed equally remote to the average citizen. Thus by arranging his items on the bill, Melville was also posing a question: What could the story of one solitary citizen possibly have to do with the big and violent doings of the world? When you ask a question like that, the answer, naturally, is: everything. But you have to prove it. The connections among Ishmaels, Afghans, and presidents are rarely seen until too late, least of all by the Ishmaels who go about their solo businesses deliberately to avoid the big and violent doings.

Ishmael minimized the significance of his adventure, yet that turned out to offer as grand a contrast, as bloody a battle, as any. In fact, it turned out to be the essential journey—the pursuit of the nemesis. It was not Ishmael's nemesis being pursued, but he was on the ship, as tied to the pursuit as if he had dreamed it up himself. If Ishmael learns anything from his mad ride with Captain Ahab, it is that no performance is solo, that the one thing you may be sure of is that every human decision, no matter how slight or peculiar, is within reach of every other such decision— as near as Afghanistan.

Call us Ishmael. Before us these days are two separate pursuits of a nemesis, one in the grand contested election, the other in Afghanistan. The lesser pursuit is Teddy Kennedy's, lesser because he is unlikely to win, and so the pursuit, while sincere, has a built-in governor. You watch the senator on television and your sympathy goes out to him. Mine does. He laughs too loud at his own jokes. The jokes are feeble, the slogans faint. He shows no compulsion to gain what he seeks, except, of course, the family compulsion that shouts, "Go to it, Teddy," which Teddy does, but without heart, without the heart of an Ahab, certainly. When he loses, then down in the public mind will go the taunting connection of the Kennedys with the presidency, and for them that will be all to the good.

But the Russians are something else, as they are always something else. You may say it's inaccurate to call Afghanistan Russia's nemesis, since the historical antagonism has always been Russia's. Yet oppressors make antagonists out of those who sit still. Now, at long last, Russia ends its frustration, giving the lie to the adorable Mishka bear, pulling on its "Potemkin" boots and pawing geniuses in the streets of Moscow. It claims that its target is limited, but so did Ahab. Older and wiser, the world knows a great white whale when it sees one, especially when the whale is the world.

So the world prepares itself, stiffens. It knows in a purely moral sense that the end of the pursuit of the nemesis always spells disaster for the pursuer, but in this case that is no consolation. Legislators call for war; panic accompanies determination; and gold goes up and down, creating an image of mammonism not seen since Mammon. So much for the extensive performances.

In the middle of all this, meanwhile, are you and I, with our solos and interludes. I have no gold to sell. My daily voyages take me to the post office, the general store, and other places whose adamant serenity tries to persuade us that we are in control of Providence. Yet there was Ishmael, calmly explaining his decision to go to sea, fully aware that life could be tied to people with dark passions striding purposefully into hell.

{ column in *The Washington Post* }

From the Unpublished Memoir
Unaccompanied Minor

Dark, dark. Today in a Fourth Avenue bookstore, I buy Rilke's *Letters to a Young Poet,* though I do not know Rilke's work, and only guess that he's a poet by the fact that he has written these letters. It is pouring, and I have neither hat nor umbrella. Unsuccessfully, I try to protect my brown wrapping paper from the slanting rain. At home in my room, I place the sodden book on newspaper, and wait two days for the pages to dry and separate. One morning, I turn a page, and a sentence rises, as if during a séance, insisting that I read it: "Therefore, dear sir, love your solitude, and try to sing out with the pain it causes you."

On the Other Hand, Writer, Rejoice

On the other hand, writer, rejoice. The heat from the fire has blistered the blue paint on your door, and the ashes from the volcano are floating like chicken feathers everywhere, and the mouth of the earthquake has swallowed up the silver and the books, and as soon as the tsunami arrives, there will be nothing left—no piano, no red vase from Italy, no antique Shaker shovel, no tennis trophy—not even a photo ID to tell you who you are.

But this, I will remind you, is what you wanted—to be free of possessions, to reflect on the worthiness of life, to be as noble as the heart allows. And, ID or no, you know who you are.

{ from the essay collection *Anything Can Happen* }

From the Book-length Essay
The Book of Love

Early in his composing career, Cole Porter visited George Gershwin to ask his advice. Porter couldn't sell his songs. Gershwin told him to make them "more Jewish," meaning that Porter should include a greater number of minor chords in his pieces to deepen the feeling toward sadness or melancholy. The results were "Night and Day," which goes minor in the third repetition of the first note; "The Still of the Night"; "Every Time We Say Goodbye" (noting "how strange the change from major to minor"); and most everything else Porter wrote after consulting Gershwin. The lyrics and the minor chords work together to say, in effect, that the true philosophy of life, and love, consists of courage with resignation. The lover is wracked with doubt when he asks, "Do you love me as I love you? Are you my life to be, my dream come true?" Yet he asks the question anyway, on the frail, brave hope that the answer will be yes.

Courage with resignation is the theme of Thomas Gray's "Elegy Written in a Country Church Yard," too. It's said that the poem is about disappointment, unrealized fame, and ambition—the flowers blushing unseen, the mute, inglorious Miltons buried in the obscure country cemetery. I don't think it's about disappointment at that level. I think the poem goes much wider and deeper, to praise the human courage to go on when, at the same time, one is resigned to failure. To such courage one pays "the tribute of a sigh." For it is not just the paths of glory that lead to the grave. Everything leads there. Knowing that, what should the noble life consist of but the courage to sing at the wall of defeat? We live at our best in a minor key, in the chill, still of the night.

From the Play
Ashley Montana Goes Ashore
in the Caicos

How to live in the world. These instructions come in French and Japanese as well, and in other languages, but don't let that throw you. Don't let anything about the enterprise throw you. You can do it, anyone can do it, because one really doesn't live in the world when it comes down to it (and it always comes down to it). Rather, one waits for the world to live in you—as a composer waits for rapture, and then becomes the life he seeks.

But, if that sounds a bit abstract to you, a little hoity-toity, read that part of *Specimen Days* in which nurse Walt Whitman is attending the Union fallen and near-dead in the U.S. Patent Office in Washington, DC, which doubled as a hospital during the Civil War—where he notes, with barely a critical remark, that the same species capable of coming up with the most dazzling inventions made of wood and brass was just as capable of blowing off one another's limbs. The hall was filled with bright shining machines side by side with men on cots, massaging their new stumps.

It is the way you feel when listening to national politicians speak of our great power and our powerful greatness, while in your heart, you recall that still and airless afternoon in Africa, when you held an eleven-year-old in your arms shortly after he had died of starvation. Light as a feather. His last breath went out of him like a drop from a vial.

So, how to live in the world? Wait till the end of the day, when the family of swans has sequestered itself under the drawbridge near the no wake sign, and the light has stalled above the open mouth of the creek, so that the sun burns like a coal in ash, and the wind is a rumor on your face, your limbs, and you are filled with wonder and remorse.

Then go treat the wounded.

A Girl Sits Weeping

W atch them. Watch the strangers. They are your character studies, your artist's models. Begin early in life, so that you can hone the skill of observing people without their knowing it. The most important thing a writer can do is to make the reader see. See the strangers.

A girl sits weeping in Columbus Circle. I am eleven. She is, what—twenty? I watch her from across the street. She sits on a stone step below the marble Columbus, and near a pedestal with an angel holding a globe. Her head is held high, as if she is looking for someone or for something. But she weeps. The effect is curious. Usually people weep with their heads in their hands. They want to hide their weeping from the world, out of shame or embarrassment, or simply out of a sense of privacy. But this girl—slight, in an old-fashioned yellow gingham dress and with a mass of red hair—she announces her tears to everyone who passes by. She publishes her sorrow, forcing people to guess why she is weeping.

She has just been fired from her job as a salesgirl as Saks. Caught ogling the cashmere sweaters, instead of waiting on customers. She was yelled at in the street by her best friend, who called her self-centered. She's broke. A thief snatches her purse in front of the Plaza, and all her money in the world is gone. Every last cent. Her lover. That's it. Her lover has left her for a magician's assistant in Newark.

A man. Or her father has disinherited her, and thrown her out of the house, with nothing but a yellow gingham dress.

Her weeping gives no hint as to which of these possibilities, if any, is the cause of her distress. And it does not abate. If anything, her tears increase, to a point where people become alarmed to look at her. Finally, a man approaches and asks her if he can be of any help. She looks at him with gratitude but keeps weeping. No. She shakes her head. No. But thank you. I wonder if she will ever stop. I start to go to her. She sees me, and gives a little don't-bother wave, and a shrug, as if to say, this is what I do—I weep.

{ from the unpublished memoir *Unaccompanied Minor* }

From the Novel
Thomas Murphy

As a poet, I have to believe in God, though I have little affection for the God I believe in and he has none for me, none that he shows, anyway. Yet I must believe, or I could not write words, structure, anything. The whole process of writing a poem is mystical, to me at least, mystical and beyond my reach. Have I told you about this? I begin a poem with an image out of nowhere (where did that come from?), and at once suspect I am part of a plan, and the poem I've begun is part of a plan. The process of writing, then, is the progression toward someone else's design. And who could that someone else be but God. It's why, I think, whenever a poet arrives at the end of a poem, the moment is always unsatisfactory, a letdown. But there you are, nonetheless, sweating like a pig and breathing hard, and knowing you've tried your hardest to fulfill what was decreed, preordained. And, of course, you've failed.

It's why I tend to write simple poems with rocks in them. I have throes of fanciness in me—I have to beat them down sometimes—but generally I dismiss them as fake thinking, as fiddling with knowledge or language for the silly sake of doing it. I know that dandyism does not make for real poetry. Arse poetica. This comes from my da, too. He could not stand waste. Of time or behavior or language. He'd tell me, Most talk is horseshit, but not as useful. So he always spoke in a straightforward way, putting one word in a slot where a lesser man would have stuffed three. Thus every word he said was, to me, beautiful.

There is a connection between this simplicity and my feeling that a poem of mine has been written before I write it, that I am tracing the original drawing, the way children trace. And, in that same way, the tracing is different from the drawing beneath it, even if it follows the lines as carefully as the child is able. As a poet, there is always something uniquely yours in a traced work, something your own that even the original artist may not have divined. Like those copyists of the Old Masters who were compelled to leave a clue that they, mere copyists, existed too. And to reach that point in a poem, it is best to keep the language simple, like my da's, so as not to muck the thing up.

What happens, then, even though you know you have failed to follow the plan perfectly, is that you've done something worthwhile on your own, imperfectly. You have kept it simple, but it is not simple. The poem has taken you to the edge of the sea, to the point where the vast sea is revealed. And though you know you cannot re-create the sea, with all its welts and fathoms, with its treasure ships half buried in the sand on the bottom, among the kelp, and its killing fish and its killing winds and manacles, still, you have brought yourself to the brink of revelation on that shore. And the beginning of revelation is, for all intents and purposes, revelation.

You never crash if you go full tilt. It takes a kind of courage to write a poem—my ma's and da's courage, and Cait's courge, and Oona's, when she was certain she was doomed, and Sarah's courage, too, when she was little and knew that she had to live all her coming days in the dark and yet got on with it. The courage to gun it, even though you're predetermined to fail. Because between that certainty and the attempt to refute it is life, boyo—dreadful, gorgeous life.

From the Memoir
Making Toast

L ate in February, I have a literary public conversation
with Alice McDermott as part of a series at the 92nd
Street Y in New York. Alice and I sit in chairs angled
toward each other on a large stage in an auditorium. Hun-
dreds of people look up at us. Usually, I feel comfortable at
such events, more so than in less heightened social situations, because when you're at the center of a public event,
you're alone. This being my first time in public after my
daughter Amy's death, however, I feel tense and out of
place. Alice's gentleness and thoughtfulness put me at ease.

We talk about *After This,* her novel about the Keane
family, whose son is killed in Vietnam. The novel centers not on death but rather on the family's grief, which
challenges their faith in God. I ask Alice what God has to
do with it. Isn't life just luck, good and bad? She says we
have to believe in God's overarching good will. "Even as
we have unbearable sorrow," she says, "small things happen that make us able to bear it. John and Mary Keane face
the greatest tragedy that a couple could face, and yet things
happen in their lives that bring them back to moments of
joy." Alice ascribes such moments to God's benevolence. I
cannot tell if she sees that I do not.

Thanksgiving Inventory

Driving on the highway, I am stuck behind a delivery truck from East Coast Custom Car. On the back of the truck, in bright yellow lettering is a list of things sold at East Coast Custom Car: stereos, alarm systems, bed liners, 4x4 accessories, trailer hitches, fog lights, wheels, "and so much more." I make a note to include these items in my accounts, then turn off toward the bay, which is winter blue already. The powerboats are wrapped and stacked. The cormorants swarm in a black mass near the mouth of a creek, their snakeheads craning for invisible killifish. I watch for a while, slip in a CD of André Previn playing "The Second Time Around," and add these things to my list as well.

Then I drive home, where I make more entries still. In the mail are new pictures of the grandchildren taken by my wife, Ginny, who is away visiting them. I share a dish of cold mashed potatoes with the dog; the wind kicks up; the fat pine on the front lawn struts in place in the late afternoon; shadows smudge the hedges; day hook-slides into night. I think of high school baseball, then basketball. The Spaldeen moon hangs so low, it looks as if it is about to fall to earth and bounce.

This inventory is getting out of hand. Last week alone I made more than a thousand new entries, and I never erase the old ones. If this keeps up, I will require a dozen ledgers, and even then my accounts will be woefully incomplete. Every year it is the same. I prepare my inventory for Thanksgiving, to say grace, and always come up short.

In a different season, W. D. Snodgrass wrote "April Inventory," an ambling elegiac list consisting mostly of the things he had gladly failed at. His poem ends on the lines "There is a loveliness exists, / Preserves us, not for specialists." Specialists were the target of his complaint. The successful people around him had zeroed in on particular and limited interests and had been rewarded for the categories they had made of their lives, while he, in unsuccessful contrast, had flopped about and picked up a few scattered items of value, like loveliness and the ability to love. My inventory is sort of like that. It is a record of haphazard events, the serendipity that Jane Jacobs used to say made for a pleasant city. So I jot down the stuff I bump into, or that bumps into me—life's precious accidents good and bad, ridiculous, astonishing. The task is overwhelming.

Did you know that there is a species of turtles called Kemp's ridley, which are born on a nesting beach in Mexico (only a few survive the hungry bird attacks) and then swim madly out to sea, where they are carried by the Gulf Stream all the way up to Long Island, New York (it takes three to five years), where they feed for a year on the defenseless spider crab as a training exercise before they take off again and swim down to the Chesapeake Bay area in Maryland, where they eat the much tougher blue claw crab for which the Long Island boot camp has prepared them? Needless to say, they made my inventory. As did the deer, the full-size antlered stag I saw the other day at dusk, as I was walking down the main street of our village. He stepped out of a driveway, as if he'd stepped out of a dream, looked about to panic, saw it was only me, and trotted, head high, down the center of the street.

Lives this month: two new young friends get married on the beach. Two brave old friends fight cancer. Another attempts to resist a deteriorating muscle disorder. Deaths this month: the philosopher Isaiah Berlin; Victor Mills, the father of the disposable diaper; and Francine Katzenbogen, a lottery winner who lavished her millions on her many beloved cats. Miss Katzenbogen died of an asthma condition severely aggravated by her cats. Cross reference: Katzanbogen/cats.

The moon is sky-high now, a small pale eye at the top of the dark. A light plane blinks overhead. A letter from a friend, a photographer, whose child is gravely ill. He includes a picture of the boy. In a corner is the photographer's shadow, like spilled ink. Too many loved ones in distress this Thanksgiving, too many entries of that sort. In adversity they conduct themselves like soldiers. A sleepless night. A new day full of migrating ducks and edible smells from the kitchen. I am ill-prepared again, but I give it a shot.

Thank you for this sublime mess. For human courage and for turtle courage. For newlyweds, cormorants, philosophers, photographers, Miss Katzenbogen, André Previn, disposable diapers, moons, dogs, deer, trailer hitches, fog lights, wheels, and so much more.

{ essay in *Time* magazine }

From the Novel
Thomas Murphy

Into the same night I walk as I did as a child, welcoming the same defeats, desires, usurpations. This irrevocable pilgrimage. As one says after a good conversation with a friend, where did the time go? Emerging from At Swim-Two-Birds, I battle a snootful. Grim kids swagger on Eighty-seventh and Columbus. A wintry creature, his keen animal's face shining in the hoarfrost, takes command of the curb. I know him from the church shelter where I teach a poetry workshop to my homeless beauties once a month. Murph! he cries. Arthur! I cry. He is huge, made of heavy curves and rounded edges. Arthur the Bear! Nobody knows if he's black or white, his skin is so caked with soot. Murph the Bard! He's in a good mood tonight. You can tell when he's not. Dr. Reynolds, the minister at the shelter, the only clergyman I've ever known with a sense of humor, calls Arthur a bi-polar bear. Murph! Arthur and I greet each other as if at sea.

All is in decline. Empires, literacy, gaudy birds. I follow a trail of rotting flowers from the Koreans' convenience store to a snowy ravine where ice has seized the upper boughs. My teeth clench. One of these days I'm going to learn to hold my liquor. One of these days I'm going to learn to hold my self-recriminations. S'long, Murph! See you, Arthur! Show me the way to go home.

Why did I not write Snodgrass? It was 1975, and he'd liked a poem of mine in the *Antioch Review*. I cannot recall why I did not write him back. Snodgrass. Poet of "Heart's Needle" and "April Inventory." Poet of quiet dread and silver maples. I have come to a stage of self-recriminations when one wonders not why one did certain things in a life but rather why not. And all the things not done are almost always the easy things, requiring the least amount of effort. Life defined by the loss of casual opportunities. Small beer. Why did I not write Snodgrass? To thank him. To gush. To tell him, if only some day, one day, even if by dumb luck, I could write a line like "my lady's brushing in sunlight," well, I'd die happy. We had a friendship in the offing. I offed it. I was stunned. Was that it? I was scared. Was that it? I was a cocky bastard, thinking, *of course* he likes my work. Why *shouldn't* he? We're *equals,* Snodgrass and I. Two peas in a poem. Was that it? Why did I not write Snodgrass?

What Should We Lead With?

J ournalists put the question in practical terms: What
should we lead with? The rest of the population sees
it more generally: What matters most? It comes to the
same puzzle. Survey events in a given period of time and
try to come up with the single moment, the headline, by
which the world may be characterized, stopped in its spin.
In the past couple of weeks, the press has stood chest-high
in choices. In Lebanon: one more last battle for Beirut; the
disintegration of the Gemayel government; the pullout of
the US Marines. In the Soviet Union: the death of Yuri
Andropov and the succession of Konstantin Chernenko; a
funeral in red. In Iowa: the small beginnings of an American presidential election; the first funny hats and toots of
the horns. In Sarajevo: one more Winter Olympics done;
memories on videotape; the ice dancers Torvill and Dean
synchronized, as if accidentally, like birds in a wind. Four
major acts, then: war, ceremony, process, grace.

What should we lead with? What matters most? Let us
concede from the start that the problem is subjective, that
whatever choice we settle on will be formed more by habit
than by a command of history; the press is not in control of history. Bored with Beirut? It's not unheard of (if
you don't live there). Every few weeks another upheaval;
the familiar picture of a crushed Mercedes, a balcony split
open like stale cake. One hears that the American people
are growing tired of the Middle East as a whole. Too bad.

The region matters, it's a lead. Boring or not, Beirut may be the center of the world, the place where everything comes together or apart.

So, too, for Moscow these past two weeks. After the obsequies and the miles of citizen mourners, half the world closes ranks behind another mystery. Who is this Cherneko, Brezhnev's former water boy turned master of the house? After Iowa, who is Mondale? Walter, we thought we knew you, but now we'd better look a bit closer at him who may become the leader of the other half of the world. Which leaves us with Sarajevo, the least important place on our current events map. Perhaps. But before we say so definitely, play it again, that ice dance performed by the two Brits. I don't think that I caught it all the first time. I think I missed one of the turns of her head, or an extension of his arm, the way they came together or apart.

Here's what one would like to say: that Torvill and Dean's routine was more important in its sublimity than all the shootings and elections time can muster; that life is short and art is long; and that the skating dance, brief and evanescent as it is, represents a perfection in which the entire universe may be encompassed. Theodore Roethke described such an effect in a poem: "A ripple widening from a single stone / Winding around the waters of the world." Nice. It may even be true. Yet it is just as likely that Beirut is the widening ripple by which everything is framed.

What we confront in making such choices are not the events alone, but ourselves; and it is ourselves we are not able to place in order. The mind, as fickle as a southern belle, swishes rapidly from battles to dances, enthralled equally with every suitor, enthralled with itself. Tell me a story about my mind, Mr. News. Did I overturn a government this week? Did I come to power? Did I win an election? Did I skate flawlessly again? Was I murderous, decorous, triumphant, beautiful? And if I was all those things, how should I order my priorities so as to know what is truly human, the essential prevailing act? The question is not what the press decrees in this week's news. The question is us. What should we lead with? What matters most?

In another poem, Roethke suggested that the widening ripple is ourselves:

I lose and find myself in the long water; I am gathered together once more;

I embrace the world.

We do that every week, cursing and awestruck at all we are.

{ essay in *Time* magazine and on *PBS NewsHour* }

The News About Jessica

The news is about Jessica, our first grandchild (have a cigar; no, don't), who was born on March 1, just under 7 pounds and 19 inches big. I hold her on the couch as she sleeps swaddled—part baby, part blanket—in the crook of my arm. Her harpist's fingers twitch in independent dreams. The threads of blue veins above her barely visible eyebrows run like rivers on a map. It comes back to you, holding babies—the surprisingly substantial weight.

The news is also about Jessica literally, in that as she sleeps, the news is on TV. As I hold Jessica, fifteen-year-old Charles Andrew Williams sits in the back of a police car that is about to take him to a county juvenile facility for killing two fellow students in Santee, California. His skin looks smoother than a baby's.

I casually realize that part of my grandfatherly duties will be to hold Jessica safe from the news, but the thought is too easy. She will also need to be alert to the news. When she is old enough, I will inform her that I am in the news business—or on the soft edges of it—and she may ask what the news business is. I will tell her that it has to do with knowing and understanding what is going on in the world.

If she demands more, of course, I will be forced to let her know that I have never understood most of the news— not the child killings, the tribal slaughters, the religious wars, the categorical hatreds, the fate of the poor, the diseased, the driven from their homes. I have never understood the weather. Not that these deficiencies have stood in the way of my sonorous brayings about the nature of the universe.

You see, Jessica, the reason that America makes guns available to children is . . . It's this way, Jessica: Some people live in the slums, and others live on the hills, and this is because . . . Look here, Jessica: The market goes up and the market goes down, and the explanation is . . . She is smiling now, an involuntary reflex.

Lest she laugh in my face, I should tell her that there are other kinds of news I do understand. The news of the heart's surprises, for example. And I should also tell her about the news of the obvious truth. That took me decades to learn. As a young writer, I was the dandiest, cleverest wit and wise guy—a cinch if one possesses the meager gifts. And then after witnessing enough pain and plain courage in the world, I simply reversed course and started writing about the life before my eyes.

Eventually one understands that the world is largely made up of obvious truths, lying in the open, begging to be repeated.

So I should also tell her about the news of the familiar, which is always strange. And the news of the routine and continuous, which is always shocking.

I should tell her about the news of the just and the good. I should relate the story of Billings, Montana, which in the Christmas season in the mid-1990s was invaded by members of the Klan and other subhumans. The intruders knocked over headstones in the Jewish cemetery, tormented an old black minister in his church, painted swastikas on the homes of Native Americans. Then they tossed a cinder block through a Jewish child's window, which was signified by a menorah. So the local paper printed up a full-page picture of a menorah, which the predominantly Christian people of Billings placed in their windows, and soon the subhumans were kicked out. I should tell her that story.

I should tell her that there is the news of the honest broker. And the news of the fair-minded. And of the modest, the quiet, the traditional, the faithful, the harmless, the on time, the responsible, the unglamorous, the unambitious, the unchatty, the constant, and the tender.

Four friends have died of cancer in recent years, slowly and without complaint.

While they were dying, the O.J. trial came and went, Monica came and went. I should tell Jessica about the news of the dignified and the brave.

The news business, I should tell her finally, involves knowing and understanding all that goes on in the world— the gentle and the intelligent as well as the stupid and the murderous. And while I would not wish this work on her unless she wishes it for herself, still I should say that if one acknowledges the full breadth of the news, then the pursuit of it makes for a useful life.

As I hold her, a girl in Santee is attempting to find the words to buoy the spirits of a brokenhearted friend. In northeast America, we are beginning to dig out of a deep and snow-packed winter and to catch flashes of sunlight. This, I should tell her, is news of gratitude and hope—or the news about Jessica.

{ essay in *Time* magazine }

The Game Is Played Away from the Ball

I used to teach this idea to journalism students to make the point that the more interesting things in the news occur without making a big noise. The rule derives from something said by Eddie Sutton, coach of the Oklahoma State University basketball team. When Sutton was coaching Arkansas, he asked his players what they did during practice. They answered, "Dribble and shoot." Then he asked them how much time they thought that they dribbled and shot during a forty-minute game—how many total minutes they had their hands on the ball. The players guessed twelve, fourteen, fifteen minutes. Sutton told them that a more likely number was two to three minutes, and he also told them what that meant in terms of the nature of the game of basketball. "Most of the game is played away from the ball," he said, meaning defense and getting into position for a pass. In journalism, it is useful to look away from the ball because most journalists don't. They turn their heads toward a particular eruptive event and miss the continuous story, which may give a far more truthful picture. In wider contexts, people tend to do the same thing and thus, make judgments based on things that happen suddenly and explosively rather than on things that happen all the time.

Here's where this rule for aging comes in: The game is also played away from the ball when it comes to people. Do not judge others by their dramatic moments—how they may panic or become nasty or wild in a crisis—in contrast to their much different normal behavior. The people they are in repose are the people they are. The people they become in a crisis are the people they become in a crisis. If you like them better in a crisis, you might create a series of shocking events for them to respond to. But if you prefer them in the quieter moments, judge them away from the ball. Naturally, this applies to the way you would like them to look at you, too.

{ from the instruction book *Rules for Aging* }

In the Madhouse in Beirut

When the twelve bombs hit the drab, gray hospital, six people were killed and twenty wounded. Two female patients were sliced to pieces by the shrapnel. The year is 1982, spring. The Beirut hospital is for people suffering from mental and psychological diseases. Among its patients are Lebanese, Palestinians, Maronites, Druze, Sunnis, Shi'ites, and Jews. An Armenian lies curled up on the second floor landing near a lateral gap that looks like an expressionless mouth. Flies collect on his bare feet. Nearby, a young woman cannot control her body. Her arms flail, her legs buckle; she smiles sweetly with her writhing lips. An old woman sits up in bed tearing a round slice of bread to small bits and tossing them on the floor. The children are penned in a small, dark space; they smell of urine; their thighs are stained with excrement. One boy shivers, another laughs. A legless girl spoons mush into the mouth of a younger one. A woman lurches forward and shouts in English: "I am normal!"

I think of these people frequently, even now, forty years later, as I walk to the clean, free beach near my home. I think of them because I cannot help it, and I realize something that applies to writing: Be grateful for those you meet who seem the most distant from you, the strangest and most alien. They are the closest.

{ from the essay collection *Anything Can Happen* }

From the Book-length Essay
The Book of Love

You wouldn't know it, but I've been clearing out the weeds. Came upon the first inkling of a rose last Saturday, and a bee breathing in the arriving season. Soon the rest of the flowers will ignite. Why I think of kettles blowing steam beats me. Maybe it's those songs they were playing on the car radio the other day. "It Might as Well Be Spring" and "Younger Than Springtime." The road to the beach is losing its grip. Soon it will turn to sand and slide into the ocean, the way the young woman slid from a climbing rope and fell to her death in a snowy ravine in that Sylvester Stalone movie we walked out on. Eventually everything loses its grip. I may be losing mine.

I have been invited to give a reading at a college in Kentucky. I'm thinking of telling them a story I've started writing about a woman in the 1850s in Northern Vermont, who opened her front door and found her drunken husband, and who, when he stormed in demanding their little boy, and threatening them both, and clapping her on the side of the head, took a shotgun and blew his chest away, so that his head fell to his legs. She wound up in Kentucky. That's the tie-in. What do you think? Too rough? I need you in moments like this, my most exacting editor. I need you in most moments. Did you say I've got a lot to learn?

From my crazy father's head I sprang—you know that—for good and ill. I inherited the rants. You remember. Still, on the whole, madness has gone better than I anticipated.

Crazy as I get, I'm a cucumber salad compared with the army generals on TV who speak of collateral damage, as if death were a cucumber salad. Years ago, I proposed a story to my editor at *Time*—I've probably told you about this—in which I would go around the world and try to quantify war. What I wanted to do was to weigh everything that went into the preparation for wars everywhere. Every contributing item—cannon, fighter jets, tanks, cluster bombs, oak-leaf clusters, rockets, the VA hospitals, the cartridges, uniforms, the epaulets, the spit and polish, the splints and crutches. The idea was to add up all this stuff, determine the tonnage, and then speculate about a world unburdened.

My editor, a good guy, considered my proposal, and eventually said no. But I always liked wondering how light the world would feel, with all that killing material off its shoulders. Nothing left but love songs about spring, and inept writers puttering around gardens, missing their wives. And since there would be no wars, there would be no need for war photographers either, and the shutterbugs could turn their attention to the weeds, the roses, and the bees.

From the Play
Ashley Montana Goes Ashore in the Caicos

Here's what I don't like. I don't like knowing that I will have lived sixty, seventy, or eighty years as a writer without having rid the world of barbarians, tyrants, traitors, bullies, murderers, liars, thieves, crooks, and backbiters. What's more, I will not have cured all the world's diseases, from the sniffles to the Ebola virus. Neither will I have prevented droughts, floods, and earthquakes. I will not have eradicated world poverty and famine. I will not have put an end to injustice, or even to casual cruelty.

I will not have established freedom and goodwill everywhere. I will not have seen to it that everyone leads a useful and productive life and exhibits only tenderness and generosity toward others—all others. I will not have unified the races, or equalized the genders, or protected and educated the children. Nothing I will have done will have resulted in a complete world reformation. In all my sixty, seventy, or eighty years—nothing. And that's what I don't like.

You think I'm kidding.

From the Novel
Thomas Murphy

Y
ou never crash if you go full tilt. Sure. But one morning you look around, and you're the only driver on the road. You can say that has nothing to do with your attitude. You are Mario Andretti at any age, and you go go go whether others are there or not. And there are no more cigarette butts in the ashtrays, no more ashtrays, or big laughs and not a drop taken where once it was taken, and you thought you heard a cough but it was a dead limb cracking and falling, well then, all you have left is the books to stave off the obvious. That, and a few ripe berries.

Through the Christmas season, TCM shows a montage of the people in movies who have died during the year. Why do I weep at the sight of Greer Garson, Ronald Colman, Lana Turner, Elisha Cook Jr., Van Heflin, Butterfly McQueen, and Burgess Meredith? I knew them not. Yet they were part of my life, of all our lives. They made an impression. Burgess Meredith, not croaking and creaking in *Rocky,* but rather Burgess Meredith in *Winterset,* under the Brooklyn Bridge, young and yearning, with an old, crackling-cellophane voice way back then. But it's not just the movies we saw these people in. They went full tilt, you see. People in movies have to go full tilt, because their lives are compressed into 90 minutes or 120. And you realize that they, too, the gone, surveyed the scene at some point in their lives and saw all the others gone. They left the theater alone, and hunted for a cab.

What I love about being a poet is that I see the world as a poem—a thing that lives between the lines, between the nodes, as Sarah puts it. Trouble is, those spaces increase as life increases. Mystery compounds mystery. And then one afternoon you want to say to someone, Look at this. Will you? And as you say that, you glance to your right, and Oona's gone. And you glance to your left, and Greenberg has gone, too. And Máire and William soon gone. Not dead, thank goodness. But gone. They become part of the space. They add to the invisible mass. Do I want to be the last man driving, only to assess the empty world as existing between the lines?

There's much to say for space, much to say for my da's gone leg, except when there's nothing to contrast it with. Burgess Meredith. Whenever they invoke *The Twilight Zone*'s greatest hits, they trot out old Burgess, wandering the wasteland city in search of peace and quiet and something to read. When he crushes his eyeglasses underfoot by mistake, that's supposed to be the tragedy of the tale. But the tragedy comes before that, when he wanders around and no one is there. It wasn't a small tragedy— poor Burgess not being able to go into seclusion with his beloved books. It was the greater tragedy. He could not see other readers. Maybe I ought to join AARP after all, and enjoy the many benefits of membership.

My hands loosen their grip on the wheel, and I shoot forward into the empty supermarket, and out again into the empty stadium, and out again. I drive to Bethlehem, Paris, Akron. Not a soul anywhere. I drive to Tinian, whence the *Enola Gay* took off for sleeping Hiroshima. I drive the runway, now weeds and midges, built extra-long for the weight of the bomber. Nothing there. Nothing in the hospitals in Galway. Nothing in the swimming pools in Mamaroneck, or in the Belnord courtyards, either one. Nothing in the New York Public Library, not even Burgess Meredith. I blast through the stacks, going a hundred, maybe two. Look. No hands. Go Oona. Go Greenberg. Go William. Go Máire. From here you look like berries.

In memoriam, everyone. Much love.

Instructions to the Pallbearers

U se the casket for a planter. I never did like boxes. Instead, prop me up on a high place where I can face the water—a bay, not an ocean—so that boats may pass before my blind eyes, and the noise of children playing on a float may attack my deaf ears. Then leave me to rot. And, keep the worms away, if you can. Death ought to be different.

{ from the essay collection *Anything Can Happen* }

If I Sing You a Song

If I sing you a song, will you listen? Listen, the way
Gretta listens in "The Dead." Songs come and go in the
story, many of them, but it is not until Bartell D'Arcy
the tenor sings at the end of the evening that we understand what song means to Joyce, and to life. D'Arcy sings
"The Lass of Aughrin," about the death of a child—"O, the
rain falls on my heavy locks / And the dew wets my skin
/ My babe lies cold." When he sings, Gretta stops in her
tracks on the staircase. She dreams into the past, of growing up near Galway in the west of Ireland, and of the boy,
Michael Furey, who at age seventeen died for loving her.

Gabriel watches his wife listen to the singing. So
removed is she from the scene of "The Dead"—from the
small talk at the dinner party, the gossip, the politics, and
the trivial wonders of a self-contained people—that Gabriel
does not recognize her, lost in the shadows. He fails to recognize his own wife. Later that night, back at their Dublin Hotel, he asks her about the great sadness in her face.
And she tells him of this boy she loved, Michael Furey,
whose love for her was so furious and fathomless, that
he made the long walk to her house one night in the cold
rain, when he was gravely ill, because he wanted to see
Gretta again. And he died. "He died for me," Gretta tells
her husband.

When she is at last asleep, Gabriel watches her. He realizes he has not loved anyone the way Michael Furey loved,

that he has never loved at all. And the story ends with his thinking about the snow that covers Ireland that night, covering the world, and all the living and the dead. Everyone had been talking talking talking at the dinner party given by the two aunts and their niece. And the whole familiar crowd had ceded a special place of honor to Gabriel, the literary man so respected for his upright dignity, his studied generosity, who was also the best talker in the room. Even now, when he sees that his wife has been no more his than he has been hers—how swiftly her soul was born back all those years to Galway by the mere notes of a song—he recalls the toast he raised to the three women, how deftly it was crafted, how well received, and how meaningless. The dead addressing the dead.

But Gretta listens to the music. And the memory of all the passion of her life, of all the lives, fills her with tears. Scholars will tell you that this is an old trick of Joyce's.

Someone plays a tune, and the principal characters are swept up in the turbulent silence of an epiphany. Never mind all that. Simply listen to the music of the inexpressible sorrow, and of the longing to live in an essential place. In the end, Gabriel promises himself to visit the west. If I sing you a song, will you listen?

{ from the book-length essay *The Book of Love* }

258

Just a Song at Twilight

You're born. They coo and sing to you and hold you up to the light, like a watermark. You learn things or you don't. People congratulate you or they don't. You succeed or you fail or you fail and then succeed or succeed and then fall on your face. You take pleasure in Shakespeare, Vermeer, Rachmaninoff, Ella, Thelonious Monk. Then they all bore you, except Monk. You win many prizes. You win no prizes. You fall in love or you don't, but eventually you do and that person is the one for you. Or not. Someone else is the one for you. You live alone. You conclude that everyone lives alone, and call that philosophy. You no longer believe in God, but then something happens and you believe but then something else happens and you don't. You develop a surprising late-life interest in the Song Dynasty or in geology or in the Sex Pistols or in harness racing. You age and weaken. Your eyesight turns bleary, your hearing creative. You grow bitter or serene or something or each. You die. Or not. Or both.

After I finished a reading recently, a young couple approached the lectern. We thought you were dead, they said. I nodded enigmatically because they were half right. Old writers exist in a kind of gloaming, and it grows increasingly difficult to tell if we are dead or alive. My so-called vital signs would suggest that I walk among the living. "Walk" is an exaggeration, since even on my more sprightly days I urge my legs forward like Boris Karloff in *The Mummy*. But there is just as much evidence that I passed away several years ago.

My world of reference is dead (see Boris Karloff reference). My friends' world of reference is dead. In our exchanges, verbal and written, we regularly resurrect superannuated names and events, such as Judge Crater and "Oh, the humanity." The books I favor are by dead people. The singers I like are long dead, including those who covered songs originally sung by those who also are dead, as are the writers of the songs.

To be sure, I am not provably dead, just nearly departed. Yet the realm of the living recedes farther and farther from my view, and the world becomes an alien planet. The papers or TV tells me that a celebrity couple is breaking up, and that their split is a cause of tragic weeping to everyone. I know not her name or his or that they are married or why they are celebrities. A new movie stars this person and that, and the trailer tells me that I loved them both in previous movies. I never heard of the previous movies, or of the stars. I can identify nearly nothing in a recent headline encrypted in *People* magazine: "Kylie Jenner's Overdrawn Lips Inspired Honey Boo Boo When She Did Mama June's Pageant Makeup." I do not even know if I know the people I know. I received a note from a friend who asked have I met the poet Marilyn Hacker. I wrote back, I don't know. I was happy enough to recognize the name of my friend.

Writers traffic in dead things, so this in-between state of being does not arrive with a shock. It is our business to bring characters, images, and memories to life from the frozen sea within us (dead Kafka reference). This is true of our work at any age, but the older we get, the more we are aware that our word supply is dwindling. The theme and subject supply, as well. When we have said all that we have to say, hurry up please, it's time (dead T. S. Eliot reference).

Until then, we straddle the realms. Others have done this, so it's not really a big deal. Charon, the ferryman of Hades, transported the souls of the newly deceased across the rivers Styx and Acheron. Persephone, daughter of Zeus, was abducted to the underworld where she adopted the yearly schedule of spending four months among the dead and eight months among the living. Ghosts—who seem to be gaining prominence in modern literature—have always had it both ways. Technically dead, they do their scaring and consoling above ground. And, of course, Jesus is said to have died into the life of the world.

I do not presume to speak for other writers my age, but for me everything that was once adventurous and exciting about the work begins to vanish like a gambler's lucky streak (dead Irving Berlin reference). I have no interest in fame. I had a taste of fame when I was young, and it only made me uncomfortable and wary of myself. Never much taken with the life of getting and spending (dead Wordsworth reference), I am even less so now, having acquired most of the things I ever wanted, both to my benefit and regret. I have no ambitions, other than maintaining the safety and well-being of my family, my friends, and my dog. I have no interest in travel. When I was a journalist, I sometimes wrote of wars in Northern Ireland, Beirut, Cambodia, Sudan, Rwanda, and elsewhere, where the mad cruelty and sadness would temper anyone's curiosity about faraway places. Not only do I never travel, I rarely move—unless you count as motion the rising out of and settling back into my very easy chair. One day, I imagine, I'll disintegrate completely in my chair, my parts absorbed by the leather. My great grandchildren will bound into the house, yelling, Let's sit in Boppo!

Passions have cooled. Grudges retain a low flame, but the heat has gone from white to pearl gray. Self-recriminations, on the other hand, never die or fade away (dead General MacArthur reference). So impressive is the stamina of the self-tormenting human conscience that the wrongs one does in a lifetime are more vivid in old age than when they originally occurred. No number of good works outweighs them in the balance. Maybe our sins constitute the true living dead. Zombies on a loop.

Before boarding Charon's ferry, writers tend to look back to see what we have done in our writing—an advantage of published work is proof that one existed—and to determine what, if anything, we bequeath to people such as the young couple at my reading, who thought me dead. All those pages we've turned out. The slag hills of debris.

What do they come to? C. Day-Lewis said, "What old men dream / Is pure restatement of the original theme." That's true, I think. Every writer tells just one story, told over and over, that moves among the various forms of telling, and to which we return in a dogged effort to understand it. The story I am.

As for the bequest, what writers leave the world is love, love at last sight. Try as we may to walk out the door giving the world the bird and one lusty fuck-you, the nature of what we do inevitably civilizes us. Of all the arts, writing is the most expansive. And the wider one goes with one's feelings and thoughts, the more one appreciates the underlying nobility of the race, and tacitly forgives the world we probe and eviscerate. Our parting shot is love. That old Celtic tune, "Just a Song at Twilight." It laments our weariness and sorrow, yet ends with "Love's old sweet song." Love's old sweet song.

{ essay in *The Southampton Review* }

Acknowledgments

The author would like to thank the following publications for originally publishing pieces of the work contained in this book, sometimes in slightly different form: *The Atlantic, The Kenyon Review, The New Republic, The New Yorker, The New York Times Book Review, PBS NewsHour, The Southampton Review, Time* magazine, and *The Washington Post.*